Terri is right: when it com[es to] matters that affect our nati[on...] option. *Running Into the F[ire...]* [...case for] every Christian to get off the sidelines and into the game. You will feel compelled to be a part of God's plan for this great nation with every page you read.

—JENTEZEN FRANKLIN
SENIOR PASTOR, FREE CHAPEL
NEW YORK TIMES BEST-SELLING AUTHOR

In her fine book, *Running Into the Fire*, author and one-time candidate for Congress Terri Hasdorff makes a compelling case that every Christian concerned about our nation must get involved in politics. This has never been truer than today, when we see a movement in politics that not only opposes our policies but the very principles on which our nation was founded. This is an important book that should cause much soul searching among those who have shied away from politics.

—FATHER FRANK PAVONE
NATIONAL DIRECTOR, PRIESTS FOR LIFE

Terri Hasdorff has written the quintessential guidebook for Christians wanting to get more involved in the political process, and she presents a very compelling case as to why we should. Anyone seeking to influence our country and culture for good must start with this inspirational blueprint for real and lasting change.

—KIMBERLY FLETCHER
PRESIDENT AND FOUNDER, MOMS FOR AMERICA®

This is a word in season for modern-day Daniels, Esthers, and Pauls. Indeed, twenty-first-century Christians must pray for those in authority, then vote to elect genuine, God-fearing leaders. This read-and-do book is a key.

—EVANGELIST ALVEDA C. KING
SPEAKFORLIFE.ORG

Terri Hasdorff knows the impact people of faith can make in their communities here at home and worldwide. In her compelling book, *Running Into the Fire*, she gives a call to action for Christians to think differently about their involvement in government and politics. True people of faith are needed now more than ever in the political arena, and this book will provide you with the information and tools necessary to know how to make a difference.

—KEN SANDE
AUTHOR OF *THE PEACEMAKER*

I have known Terri from our days fighting for conservative principles in the US House, and she understands how important it is for people of faith to get involved in politics. Christians have been shamed out of politics, and that must end. Terri's book tells us what we can do.

—MATT SCHLAPP
CHAIRMAN, AMERICAN CONSERVATIVE UNION

Terri Hasdorff has presented a very strong and compelling case for American Christians to be faithful citizens and get involved in what most call "politics"; however, the Bible calls it "ministry." The self-governing we have been blessed with in the United States of America brings with it a duty to participate, and *Running Into the Fire* is a strong call for all faith-based citizens to do their part.

—REV. DAVE WELCH
PRESIDENT, US PASTOR COUNCIL

RUNNING INTO THE FIRE

TERRI HASDORFF

Most Charisma Media products are available at special quantity discounts for bulk purchase for sales promotions, premiums, fund-raising, and educational needs. For details, call us at (407) 333-0600 or visit our website at www.charismamedia.com.

RUNNING INTO THE FIRE by Terri Hasdorff
Published by FrontLine, an imprint of Charisma Media
600 Rinehart Road, Lake Mary, Florida 32746

This book or parts thereof may not be reproduced in any form, stored in a retrieval system, or transmitted in any form by any means—electronic, mechanical, photocopy, recording, or otherwise—without prior written permission of the publisher, except as provided by United States of America copyright law.

Unless otherwise noted, all Scripture quotations are taken from New International Version®, NIV®. Copyright © 1973, 1978, 1984, 2011 by Biblica, Inc.® Used by permission of Zondervan. All rights reserved worldwide. www.zondervan.com. The "NIV" and "New International Version" are trademarks registered in the United States Patent and Trademark Office by Biblica, Inc.®

Scripture quotations marked KJV are from the King James Version of the Bible.

Scripture quotations marked NKJV are taken from the New King James Version®. Copyright © 1982 by Thomas Nelson. Used by permission. All rights reserved.

Copyright © 2022 by Terri Hasdorff
All rights reserved

Visit the author's website at www.Godovergovernment.com.

Cataloging-in-Publication Data is on file with the Library of Congress.

International Standard Book Number: 978-1-63641-167-5
E-book ISBN: 978-1-63641-168-2

While the author has made every effort to provide accurate
internet addresses at the time of publication, neither the
publisher nor the author assumes any responsibility for errors
or for changes that occur after publication. Further, the
publisher does not have any control over and does not assume
any responsibility for author or third-party websites or their
content.

22 23 24 25 26 — 987654321
Printed in the United States of America

This book is dedicated to all Christians brave enough to leave the stands, step into the arena, and serve.

Government is not reason; it is not eloquence—it is force!
Like fire, it is a dangerous servant and a fearful master;
never for a moment should it be left to irresponsible action.

—AUTHOR UNKNOWN

CONTENTS

FOREWORD

ONE OF THE most widely accepted, but clearly wrong, ideas extant among conservatives and Christians today (some of them my friends) is this: politics is downstream from culture. This popular aphorism argues that the broader culture determines the shape of politics through some kind of social derivative effect—and not the other way around. If this is true, we should not look to politics as an answer to cultural problems. Said another way: don't expect politics to get any better until the culture gets better. Let's be more direct and say what many proponents of this notion believe but seldom say out loud: elected officials should not be held responsible and accountable to fix cultural problems that are not of their making. Fix the culture and you will see politics self-correct, according to this view.

The logical failure of this "downstream" idea is twofold. First, you could just as easily say this same thing about anything—not just politics. Don't expect medical ethics to get any better because healthcare values and principles are downstream from culture. Don't expect the warp and woof of Wall Street to get any better because financial ethics are downstream from culture. Ditto education, science, the arts, entertainment, news and information, and so on.

Yet the greater logical misfiring is the idea that politics is somehow *separate from culture* rather than an integral part of it. This is the only reasonable conclusion to be made from the language of downstream and upstream. But in reality, each and every social institution is by definition an elemental portion of the broader culture. In our day, this notion of political separatism is falsified on an hourly basis as we see society permeated with political controversy—even in some areas generally viewed as apolitical. Take, for example, the sporting culture. Historically a bastion of talent, excellence, perseverance, and competitive drive, the sports world today is a giant political petri dish. Witness the seemingly endless controversies over the Pledge of Allegiance, politically correct team names, and mixed-gender athletic competitions. Sports and every other cultural institution are part and parcel of the broader culture. Politics is not downstream from culture; it is, rather, woven through the entire fabric of culture.

We can, of course, easily acknowledge that the participants in any particular cultural endeavor or enterprise are themselves individually shaped by the values of the broader culture. That is to say that in some sense all of us exist downstream from culture. But that is a mere tautology. There has never been a time in human history when that was not so. But the larger observation to be made here is not the failure of logic but the failure of will and the attempt by some to avoid the responsibility to act by arguing that someone else needs to fix the culture first.

As one of my professors used to say: "What's needed here is a little clear thinking." To get that clarity, we must look to the triumvirate of core American principles embodied in the Declaration of Independence—that all people are created equal, that their rights come from

God not government, and that the only just governments are those derived from the consent of the governed. It's this last core principle—that a just government is derived from the consent of the governed—that falsifies the entire notion of politics being downstream from culture. Politics, rightly understood, is at the core of *shaping* culture, largely through lawmaking—lawmaking with the consent and active engagement of "we the people."

The poster child of this right understanding of shaping culture through political engagement is Great Britain's William Wilberforce. At a time when the reigning political and social culture were decidedly pro-slavery (with a majority of members of Parliament taking money from the slave trade), Wilberforce and his confederates labored upstream against the culture using the medium of political action and social engagement. After decades of travail, Wilberforce and his Clapham friends prevailed, with both slavery and the slave trade being abolished in the British Empire.

The same was true in America. Both Southern plantations and Northern factories profited handsomely from the institution of slavery. American abolitionists labored against this culturally ingrained injustice through political action and social engagement. Unfortunately, it took a civil war with more than a million deaths to end slavery in America.

Politics is not the definitive answer to cultural decay. The root of this decay is primarily spiritual. Yet it is not wrong to say that politics is part of the answer—and in our day an important part. All this makes Terri Hasdorff's *Running Into the Fire* a timely and important contribution to understanding the times, to ignoring the naysayers, and to accepting personal responsibility for engaging the political culture with biblical truth. Terri gives us insights, practical training, and a plan—all of it forged in the fires of political experience and resting on a firm foundation of biblical understanding.

This book will certainly change your understanding, build your confidence, and help you listen for the quiet voice of Him who holds your future—and the future of our nation—in His hand. Be careful. It may change your life. And God may use you and others to change the world.

—Frank Wright, PhD
Chairman, National Religious Broadcasters

INTRODUCTION

There is not a square inch in the whole domain
of our human existence over which Christ, who
is Sovereign over all, does not cry, Mine!
—ABRAHAM KUYPER, FORMER PRIME
MINISTER OF THE NETHERLANDS

MANY OF THE problems we face in our country are rather unprecedented. We have never been closer to socialism, child pornography is rampant, sex trafficking is skyrocketing, the United States in 2020 recorded the largest annual increase in the murder rate in six decades,[1] and people are dying from drug overdoses at record levels.[2] California wildfires are raging out of control, burning millions of acres—the equivalent of nearly ten thousand square *miles* in 2020 and 2021 alone. The United States has the highest incarceration rate of any country,[3] and American prisons and jails house more than two million inmates, or nearly a quarter of the world's prison population.[4]

A surprising number of those prison inmates are politicians. Former congressman Billy Tauzin (R-LA) often remarked that "half of Louisiana is underwater and the other half is under indictment."[5] Former New Orleans mayor Ray Nagin served more than five years in prison for corruption.[6] Former congressman Randall "Duke" Cunningham (R-CA) pled guilty to accepting $2.4 million in bribes and served seven years in prison.[7] Kwame Kilpatrick, former mayor of Detroit, was convicted of twenty-four felony counts of mail fraud, wire fraud, and racketeering.[8] In Illinois, four former governors have gone to prison in the last fifty-five years. In Alabama, three of the past six elected governors have been convicted; and in 2020, former state House speaker Mike Hubbard began his sentence after being convicted on multiple counts of violating state ethics laws, though several of those convictions were thrown out on appeal.[9]

Lately, each headline is more shocking and heartbreaking than the last. Global COVID-19 pandemic case numbers have exceeded 530 million,[10] and wildfires in 2021 were logged as some of the worst on record, causing so much damage that the devastation could be seen from space.[11] Indeed, it seems that the whole world is on fire. So how did we get here? I've been thinking a lot about that lately. As a Christian, the question that one must ask is this: What role does the body of Christ play in all this?

We Christians have forgotten who we are. We have been deceived into thinking we are powerless. We are not! Of the more than 332 million people in the United States, 69 percent of adults identify as Christians.[12] According to a 2020 Pew Research report, "Christians account for the majority of registered voters in the U.S. (64%)."[13]

If the numbers are on our side, what do we, as believers, do? How do we fight back against a political system that seems so deeply entrenched, out of control, and often filled with volatility and hot tempers? The answer is simple: we need to remember who we are and obey what God has commanded us to do. We need to look no further than Romans 8:31: "If God is for us, who can be against us?"

Most people have no idea how much political leaders' decisions impact their daily lives. A poll conducted in 2015 showed that 77 percent of Americans ages eighteen to thirty-four could not name even one senator in their home state,[14] and according to a 2016 survey led by the Annenberg Public Policy Center, only one in four Americans surveyed can name all three branches of government.[15]

Many Americans have adopted a view that they don't need to concern themselves with government and public policy. Apathy toward the government has become acceptable. It's only when corruption, gas prices, or pure insanity rise to an exceptional level that most people take note; but even then, they shrug it off with statements like "Well, that's just how it is with politics" and "What can I, as just one person, do?" Then they go right back to their daily lives. Unless you have large sums of money to give away, you probably feel powerless to change what you see around you. Quite often, even those who contribute large amounts, I've learned, feel this way as well! It is very clear how much we have enabled our current system by not trying to understand what is really happening and not getting involved.

Recently, I found inspiration in a *New York Times* article about the methods used to fight the California wildfires. They too have become more dangerous and difficult to battle over the years. Warmer temperatures are making the forests drier and more susceptible to burning. Fires are increasing in frequency, and the fire season is lasting longer. According to the *Times*, "The basic techniques for fighting wildfires have changed little in decades.

Aircraft dropping water and chemicals from the sky, and on the ground bulldozers, adzes, chain saws and the boots of thousands of firefighters racing to hold back the flames."[16] Some of this effort includes burning areas in the path of the flames to stop their progression. Hence, the term "fighting fire with fire."

When I asked a friend why he believes Christians shy away from politics, he gave a rather profound answer. He explained that Christians are afraid to enter politics because they think of it as being dirty or corrupt. But what we really need to do, he said, "is become more like firefighters and those in the military, who are trained to overcome their fears, and instead of running *away* from the intense heat of fires…they are trained *to run right into them*." He went on to say, "Because how else can you put out the fire?" My friend is right! Christians have given in to fear, and the flames keep getting higher and higher.

When we, as the body of Christ, are not willing to run into the fire of politics, then quite often, we're leaving that job to the ones going in with the matches! We are commanded to walk by faith, not in fear. As I will explain later, true Christians are the best equipped to deal with what arises in politics if we are trained properly, yet so often, we are the last ones who want to get involved.

You and I do not have the luxury of sitting on the sidelines, watching the fires of the political process and our democracy burn out of control. As Christians, we are called to run into that fire, armed not with axes, bulldozers, and chainsaws, but with our votes, our wallets, our influence, and above all, the Spirit of God. The front lines of democracy need us.

This book is a call to action for Christians to think differently about being involved in government and politics. Evidence showing that many believers have abdicated their role in this area abounds. As my friend Aamon Ross likes to say, "If you want to see what government and politics look like without Christians involved, just turn on your TV." It seems that everything Christians believe is under attack. Socialism and Far Left policy that stifle religious freedom are taking hold more and more each day, and religious persecution is on our doorstep. This book aims to equip you with information and tools to help you make a difference and give you the hope and understanding that you *do have the power* to influence what you see happening around you.

So gear up. We are running into the fire. Together, we will not only reduce the rate of wildfires, we will restore what is beautiful in the land and what is native—the foundational values on which this country was established.

CHAPTER 1

THIS IS WHAT THEY WILL EAT

*If through a broken heart God can bring His purposes to
pass in the world, then thank Him for breaking your heart.*
—OSWALD CHAMBERS

HAVE YOU EVER experienced a life-changing
moment? A moment when you knew you would
never look at the world the same? Or maybe it was
a moment of insight that would forever eliminate your
automatic, learned responses?

For me, that moment came while visiting Kenya in
2007. After starting a new job with the US Agency for
International Development, Convoy of Hope invited me to
tour a part of Nairobi called the Mathare Valley, an area of
just three square miles inhabited by nearly 600,000 people.[1]
The poverty and tragic conditions there overwhelmed me.
The only places I could think of where conditions might
be worse were India or Pakistan. I mentioned this to our
tour leader, who had worked in both places, and he con-
firmed that very few differences existed.

Everywhere I looked, I saw orphans. Children who had
lost their parents to HIV/AIDS scrounged through the
garbage dumps searching for food. About one in three
adults in the Mathare Valley is HIV-positive, leaving children as young as eight years old to run a "household" and

care for their younger siblings.2 The children suffer from malnutrition, dysentery, malaria, and so much more.

Most of the homes, if you can call them that, were mere shacks with mud walls and tin roofs. There was no electricity, no running water, and no sewage system. It was so dangerous there and the poverty was so extreme that the police and the fire department would not respond if called. It was truly one of the closest things to a man-made hell I have ever seen on earth.

Our African guide, Rev. Peter Nuthu, had been the pastor of a large church in a wealthier part of Nairobi; then one day, he and his wife visited Mathare. His wife encouraged him to start a one-day-a-week feeding program for the children there. Quickly, they realized that this food was the only real meal many of the children had all week! So Rev. Nuthu and his wife gave up their nice home and church in the better part of town and moved their ministry to the edge of Mathare.

As we stood in the courtyard inside the gates, the reverend explained that we were going to a dangerous place because the people there were so desperate. We were instructed to leave any of our jewelry behind and to tuck our cameras inside our jackets. Then six strapping young men armed with billy clubs surrounded us to provide protection. As Rev. Nuthu led us outside the safety of his compound through a back gate, I felt like I was walking through a portal into another world.

As we walked deeper into the valley, the sights, smells, and sounds of human suffering were the most tragic I have ever witnessed or could have even imagined before my visit. Rev. Nuthu led us deeper and deeper until we reached a fetid mountain, a fifty-foot-high accumulation of garbage, excrement, and death that had been building for years. I stopped in my tracks as he started leading everyone to climb up that enormous mountain of garbage. I hung back with one of my staff members and decided to stay behind until the rest of the group returned. I did not want to go farther up because it looked so unpleasant and possibly unsafe; but Rev. Nuthu noticed I was not with them and turned back around to get me. With an almost desperate look in his eyes, he took my hand and said, "Please, come with me; I need to show you something." I mustered the courage and followed him.

We climbed for several minutes and were about halfway up when he stopped and suddenly pointed to something at his feet—a pile of rotting goat intestines that were turning black and were covered in flies. The smell made me nauseous. It was simply disgusting to even look at them. I stared at the reverend with complete bewilderment. He could see that I didn't under-

> With an almost desperate look in his eyes, he took my hand and said, "Please, come with me; I need to show you something."

stand why he was showing me this, so he looked into my eyes, pointed again with great fervor, and said, "*This is what they eat!*" I stared at him in disbelief. He said it again. "If we don't feed them, this is what the children will come and eat." My mind began to race as I understood the unbelievable horror and gravity of what he was explaining.

My instinct was to run as fast as I could from this place. Run back to my hotel, with its hot water and a bed with nice clean sheets, and then back onto the plane home. But my feet were lead, my heart was heavy, and my eyes held back tears, for that was the moment—the moment that I knew inaction was no longer an option. To shake my head and offer my meager prayers would never be enough. I knew that, just like Rev. Nuthu, I had to get involved and personally help make a difference.

Now, reflecting on that experience years later, that is exactly how I feel about the current state of American politics. While the political façade in America may not be as jolting as a slum in Africa, the reality is much more fetid than most Americans know.

CHAPTER 2

INACTION IS NO LONGER AN OPTION

Bad men need nothing more to compass their ends,
than that good men should look on and do nothing.
—JOHN STUART MILL

WHEN I RETURNED to my hotel room that night after visiting Mathare, I reflected on something that had moved me deeply when I stood next to that huge mountain of garbage in one of the worst slums in the world—and it has stayed with me ever since. In the heart of that desperate place, the *only* people I saw responding to the needs were Christians. When I looked around, I didn't see any movie stars speaking out about the injustices. I didn't see anyone from the local media. One thing stood out in a place where even the fire department and the police wouldn't respond to cries for help. The people I *did* see there, helping those in need day in and day out, were true people of faith who weren't afraid to get involved.

No matter where you are in the world, even if there is no electricity, no running water, and no real infrastructure of any kind, you can almost always find a church.[1]

I was raised in the church, and my career path is the result of continual prayer and a desire to serve. Having worked as a major gifts officer for more than one large Christian nonprofit, I have come to know personally several high-net-worth individuals, many of them deeply committed Christians. In early 2019, I attended a fundraising dinner at a beautiful hotel in downtown Washington, DC. In an elegant ballroom, I sat next to a man and his wife who have a personal net worth greater than the gross domestic product of most third world countries. The husband spent a large part of the evening lamenting to me about the state of the country, telling me at length how worried he was for his grandchildren and how he wished we could have better people in leadership right down the street at the historic buildings we were surrounded by in Washington. I listened carefully to what he and his wife said and told them I shared many of their concerns.

I had no idea that night that less than six months later, God would make it clear to me, after a great deal of prayer and fasting, that I was to run for Congress. For some time, I had held the dream of serving in public office, and suddenly such an opportunity to do just that arose. Unexpectedly, a seat was about to be vacated that had previously looked like it would remain occupied for a long time. For me, the decision came down to a question of obedience to God. I didn't know if I was supposed to win; I just knew I was supposed to run.

I filed the paperwork and hired a team of consultants and was told that if I had any hope of winning, I needed to raise at least $750,000. That amount seemed overwhelming, but because I know so many strong Christians who care deeply about the country, I firmly believed that with their help, I could raise the amount needed to be successful.

Serious questions existed about the integrity of my main opponents, and thousands of dollars were being poured into their races. The consultants believed that I had a good shot at winning *if* I could raise enough money to let people know they had a solid, honest alternative who would stand up for faith and family values. I had spent years working on Capitol Hill as a legislative staffer, and I knew how to get things done in Washington. My great desire was to put my knowledge and experience to work to help the people I would represent. But if the voters didn't even know who I was, none of that would matter.

I called the man I'd had the honor of having dinner with just a few months earlier. After excitedly explaining to him what God was leading me to do, I asked him if he and his wife would donate some of the critical funds I needed to have a real fighting chance at winning. After all, I was a Christian like him. I was highly trained, shared his values, and he and his wife knew me personally.

I almost dropped the phone when he said, "Terri, I'm sorry, but I'm not going to be able to help you. My wife and I decided a long time ago that *we just don't get involved in politics*. We only give our money to Christian nonprofits. *We don't give money to political campaigns*" (emphasis mine).

I could barely speak. I had just quit my job, taken a huge leap of faith, and committed to doing the scariest thing I have ever done. I was putting myself on the front lines to stand up for the things we both believed in at a time when those views were under withering assault. Some of my opponents were people *exactly* like the ones he had complained about just a few months earlier. They were people who seemed to lack integrity, yet he was unwilling to do anything to help me fight. I was *stunned*.

I felt my knees buckle as I weakly stammered out a

thank you for his time and hung up the phone. I couldn't believe it. As my mind raced, I thought, "Surely, this must be an isolated incident, right? Surely, plenty of other Christians will support me, especially when I have been hearing so often about how hard it is to find people who are willing to step forward and run for office, who are in it for the right reasons and are not self-serving."

I am disappointed to say that over and over, people told me, "I'm sorry; we just don't get involved in politics." This came from *strong Christians*—friends, colleagues, and people from church or Bible study groups. Many of them said things like, "Politics is just so nasty," "Everyone is so corrupt," and "You really can't change the system." And on the criticisms went. When I looked back at the end of my race, only a few solid, committed people had stepped up and said yes. Their friendship and support meant everything to me and still does. It mattered to them because they *got it*. In their minds, they were investing in the kingdom and in me. That was the paradigm shift.

I was determined to not let them down. I gave my race everything I had. My team and I left it all on the field, but unfortunately, I did not win. My opponents outspent me by hundreds of thousands of dollars, and as my consultants explained, it was a numbers game. If you don't have the money, you are almost guaranteed not to win.

In our current election system, it's all about name recognition, and in most cases, you have to buy that. My opponents had way more ability to buy it than I did. They had the money to outspend me and could pay for billboards on almost every corner of the district and for TV ads that ran constantly day and night. How could I compete with that?

After my race ended and I had some time to reflect on what happened, I was truly the most aggrieved by how incredibly hard it is for anyone to get elected who is not willing to take money from special interests. Our system seems to be slanted more and more toward candidates who are willing to compromise heavily to get money. In addition, if you have a very short lead time to raise money, as I did, how can you possibly compete with someone who can bring in millions of dollars?

And unfortunately, even if you have millions of dollars and are willing to self-fund, often you still will not win. According to OpenSecrets, congressional self-funding has skyrocketed in 2022, with candidates using their own money more "in the first year of the 2022 midterm cycle than in years past. If past self-funding is any indication, the 2022 cycle is on track to bring in possibly record-breaking amounts of self-funding."[2]

However, even though these candidates have a lot of money, many of them are still losing. OpenSecrets finds, "As the costs of running for office have escalated, more and more candidates are jumping into politics using their personal fortune, rather than trying to raise all those funds from other people. Though they don't lack for money, self-funded candidates typically lose at the polls. In the 2020 cycle, 36 candidates spent more than $1 million of their own money." Twenty-seven of those thirty-six lost their races.[3]

This data shows that money alone is not all that is needed. Unless you have a major force behind you, such as a huge amount of grassroots support or many people willing to donate, fundraise, and personally get involved in other ways, it's not possible. And that major force is what I believe God wants to stir up through the body of Christ.

I hope you will read this book and understand that in the same way that Rev. Nuthu and his wife realized they could not ignore the truth and do nothing, you as well will realize that you *must* get involved. Inaction is no longer an option. Lives depend on it. Your life and the lives of your children depend on it. If our nation continues to consume the garbage that is the fruit of corruption, selfishness, and bad decision-making because we sit back and do nothing, our country will die.

As James 2:20 says, "Faith without works is dead." Putting that faith into action is powerful. I want to help you see that you have power, a power you may not realize, to change the world, starting with your city or hometown and spreading throughout the rest of your country. Our country. One nation under God.

A few years ago, I heard a pastor tell a story about a man who had, in his last will and testament, left his home to Satan. His lawyer, who was the executor of his will, struggled for weeks with how to carry out the man's last wishes. Finally, when one of the other attorneys in his firm asked him what he would do to give the home to Satan, the attorney replied, "Absolutely nothing." His colleague was rather shocked and confused, but after a few months, he began to understand the wisdom of his coworker's statement.

Within a very short amount of time, because no one was caring for the home, the weeds and vines grew up and covered the house. Eventually, the roof began to leak, and then one day, it caved in, allowing the elements to destroy almost everything inside. The attorney realized that inaction was the most effective way to allow something of value to be destroyed and handed over to evil. The church and the body of Christ have been deceived into believing that they should stay out of politics and just do nothing. True Christians on both sides, both Republicans and Democrats, are not involved, so we see the results of the decline in morals in our government leaders more and more every day.

As Christians, we are personally responsible for government at the local, state, and federal levels. If we don't like what we see, it's our job to change it. Authentic Christians have divorced themselves from politics and government for far too long out of fear, apathy, or ignorance. We must be educated regarding what the Bible says about our involvement in government and then train and support others who want to make a difference.

> *I want to help you see that you have power, a power you may not realize, to change the world, starting with your city or hometown and spreading throughout the rest of your country. Our country. One nation under God.*

It is more important now than ever before for the body to rise up, because we are losing our freedoms, and our very right to practice our faith could be in jeopardy. Our freedom of speech is being reduced each day. With the online tech environment seemingly stacked against those with a conservative Christian viewpoint, one must ask this: Who is getting to decide what freedom of speech is? More and more, we are reading headlines about Christian censorship. Facebook, the biggest social media community in the world, with 2.9 billion active users, shut down a Christian ministry page in 2020 with no explanation given, according to Anne Paulk of Restored Hope Network.[4] In 2021, Facebook suspended a Christian professor from Houston Baptist University.[5] How many more similar cases never make the news?

You simply don't have the luxury of merely voting at the ballot box anymore. You also need to vote with your wallet, time, influence, and personal involvement. I'm going to help you learn how.

CHAPTER 3

THE POWER OF THE BODY

*Faith is taking the first step even when
you don't see the whole staircase.*
—MARTIN LUTHER KING JR.

A S I LOOK back, I realize that God has given me a
career path with some rather unique experiences.
I have built bridges at the intersection of faith
and government my whole life, and I have learned that
serving people through a role in government can be just
as important as serving them through a role in the church.

If you are a Christian, you are part of a family—a very
large family with the resources to accomplish anything
God calls us to do. The Christian community must recognize that we have the resources to change what is happening in our country, our state, and our cities. Instead
of waiting for the change, we need to *be* the change. We
cannot afford to sit back and abdicate the role of government and politics.

To be involved in our communities is also to be involved
in the political processes that impact them. Is it not better
to prevent tragedy before we must race in and help heal
it? The tragedy of corruption and betrayal of the people
is happening every day in our modern system, and we *do*
have the power to do something about it!

Many Christians have quite simply forgotten our

enormous collective power. The church is the largest, most stable, and most extensively dispersed nongovernment organization in any country in the world![1] And when I say the church, if you are a Christian, I mean you! Carey Nieuwhof, the lead pastor of Connexus Church in Barrie, Ontario, says, "If you're a Christian, church is not something you go to. It's something you are....You don't go to church. You *are* the church."[2]

As pointed out by Family Health International, "Churches are respected within their communities, and most have existing resources, structures, and systems upon which to build. They possess the human, physical, technical, and financial resources needed to support and implement small- and large-scale initiatives. They can undertake these actions in a very cost-effective manner due to their ability to leverage volunteers and other resources with minimal effort."[3]

Pastor Rick Warren writes about how the church is "the greatest force on the face of the Earth." It provides the "highest motivation" and the "strongest authorization" because as Christians, "we love God, and our love for God compels us to love other people. It is love that never gives up; it is love that keeps moving forward despite the appearance of impossible odds, and it is love that outlasts any problem....When you know that God has authorized you to do something, you don't worry about failure....In fact, the Bible teaches that God will give us his power to complete the task. This is God's way—ordinary people empowered by his Spirit."[4]

The United States has the largest Christian population

in the world and, more specifically, the largest Protestant population globally, with more than 200 million Christians.

According to researcher George Barna, in the 2016 presidential election: "Donald Trump would have lost by a landslide had a significant slice of the voting populace—conservative Christians who are active both spiritually and politically—not turned out and voted for him in overwhelming numbers....A survey conducted the week after the election by the Cultural Research Center at Arizona Christian University discovered that among SAGE Cons—an acronym for Spiritually Active Governance Engaged Conservative Christians—99% turned out to vote. That nearly universal turnout level dwarfed the estimated national turnout level of 66%, which itself was above-average. But just as remarkable as their turnout was the solidarity of the segment's vote: 97% of SAGE Cons cast their ballot for President Trump.

"To place that unity in context, the national exit polls show the highest levels of solidarity among other population segments to include Democrats (94% voted for Joe Biden), Republicans (94% voted for Donald Trump), black women (90% for Biden), liberals (89% for Biden), blacks (87% for Biden), and conservatives (85% for Trump). However, none of those segments had a turnout level approaching that of SAGE Cons. SAGE Cons represent 9% of the adult population but their extreme level of turnout enabled them to constitute slightly more than 14% of the voting population. In raw numbers, there were approximately 23 million SAGE Con votes cast. With 97% of those going to Donald Trump, the SAGE Con bloc provided the president with a net margin of more than 21 million votes."[5]

The same is true for the election of former President George W. Bush. "Had it not been for the unusually high turnout among voters driven by religious convictions, the results might have been different," according to the Barna Group.[6]

This shows the enormous power of engagement! You *do* have the power to influence change in government. Imagine what will happen if the body of Christ begins to really walk in that power.

Some simply do not believe that politics is something Jesus would call them to do, so they take no action other than prayer. But the truth is, He has given us the authority and ability to govern. The truth is that the government is designed for moral people to run it.

To quote one of our Founding Fathers, John Adams, "Our Constitution was made only for a moral and a religious people. It is wholly inadequate to the government of any other."[7] If moral people do not run our system, it undermines our Constitution. If our elected leaders are only guided by their selfish ambitions, quite often they will fail to make moral decisions.

I am reminded of Matthew 7:3–5, "Why do you look at the speck of sawdust in your brother's eye and pay no attention to the plank in your own eye? How can you say to your brother, 'Let me take the speck out of your eye,' when all the time there is a plank in your own eye? You hypocrite, first take the plank out of your own eye, and then you will see clearly to remove the speck from your brother's eye."

It is time to get the plank out of your eye when it comes

to political involvement. Before you complain about the problems you see with the government, ask yourself, "What am I doing to get involved and make a difference?" Everyone can do something. To have a moral, efficiently running political system is as important as having clean water and healthy food.

Professor Arthur Brooks of Harvard Business School has conducted numerous research studies. He finds that civic engagement data shows "religious people are 25 percentage points more likely than secularists to give money (91 percent to 66 percent) and 23 points more likely to volunteer their time (67 percent to 44 percent)." He discovered that the more serious the religious engagement—for example, regular worship service attendance—the higher the level of charitable commitment.[8] Christians understand the concept of tithing, but they seem to be totally disconnected from the fact that just as money is needed to run a church and feed orphans, money is needed to run campaigns to elect the *right* kind of people to office.

We face a decline in Christian values that is driven, in many cases, by our own government, and the church has largely stood by and watched. While churches must follow certain guidelines to comply with the IRS, a profound lack of understanding has existed in this area for centuries. I have included an entire section in the back of this book with a list of organizations you can reach out to for more information on what the church can and cannot do. Ignorance and fear are the enemies of the church fulfilling its call in this area.

I have seen firsthand that people of faith can make an incredible difference in the needs of suffering communities here at home and all over the world. I have witnessed them fighting problems such as homelessness, youth violence, drug addiction, HIV/AIDS, and malaria. I have seen them respond to disasters, provide education, deliver food assistance, and so much more. That degree of caring, commitment, and organization can also work toward strengthening our democracy and governance.

First and foremost, we must humble ourselves and pray, for this should always be where we start. "If my people, who are called by my name, will humble themselves and pray and seek my face and turn from their wicked ways, *then* I will hear from heaven, and I will forgive their sin and *will heal their land*" (2 Chron. 7:14, emphasis added).

> To have a moral, efficiently running political system is as important as having clean water and healthy food.

It doesn't stop there however. Saying to our leadership, "I'm going to pray for you," and then going on about our lives just isn't enough. To restore the country and preserve our freedoms, including our religious freedoms, *you* are going to have to get involved.

What would have happened if Elisha stopped with prayer in 2 Kings 4:32–35? "When Elisha reached the house, there was the boy lying dead on his couch. He went in, shut the door on the two of them, and prayed to the Lord. Then he got on the bed and lay on the boy, mouth to mouth, eyes to eyes, hands to hands. As Elisha stretched himself out on him, the boy's body grew warm. Elisha turned away and walked back and forth in the room and then got on the bed and stretched out on him once more. The boy sneezed seven times and opened his eyes." Prayer was just the start of the miracle that was performed through Elisha!

We pray first that we are guided to make the right choices at the polls. Too often we blindly vote for the career politician because we recognize their name. Are we biased just because we've heard about them for years, sometimes most of our lives? But what do we really know about them? Are they serving the people who sent them there? Many of these folks are good at getting elected, but they are not very good at serving their constituents. Perhaps you feel like God has been nudging you to get more involved politically or to even consider running for office. Are you concerned about what you see happening around you but don't know what to do? Thinking differently about how you approach the arena of government may be what God is encouraging you to do.

CHAPTER 4

SENDING DANIEL INTO THE LIONS' DEN

Now when Daniel learned that the decree had been published, he went home to his upstairs room where the windows opened toward Jerusalem. Three times a day he got down on his knees and prayed, giving thanks to his God, just as he had done before. Then these men went as a group and found Daniel praying and asking God for help. So they went to the king and spoke to him about his royal decree: "Did you not publish a decree that during the next thirty days anyone who prays to any god or human being except to you, Your Majesty, would be thrown into the lions' den?"

—DANIEL 6:10–12

W HAT IF WE are faced with so many problems in our society because the people of faith who have been called to serve in government have been disobedient? What if they have ignored the call on their lives due to fear or other reasons, and what we see around us is the fruit of that decision? Jesus made it clear that those who are obedient are His disciples (John 8:31). If you are truly a Christian, you strive to be obedient and to know and follow the teachings and example of Jesus Christ. What if obedience to God is serving in politics?

With recent worldwide events, it has been said that we

are living in an age of "existential fear."[1] But fear is the absence of faith.

Many Christians are afraid of going into politics because they fear becoming corrupt. Although this is a healthy fear, we as Christians are not encouraged to shy away from other professions that have the potential for corruption or danger. So why avoid the political arena? And, as in all things we do, are we not called to walk by faith?

Psalm 91 is a treasured Bible passage to many, but let's look at something you may not have noticed in verses 1–3.

> Whoever dwells in the shelter of the Most High
> will rest in the shadow of the Almighty. I will say
> of the LORD, "He is my refuge and my fortress, my
> God, in whom I trust." Surely he will save you from
> the fowler's snare and from the deadly pestilence.
> —PSALM 91:1–3

One day while reading this passage, I felt prompted to go and look up the definition of *pestilence*. If you are like me, you have probably read this passage a hundred times and never paid much attention to that word; but do you know that the word *pestilence* has a broader definition than just meaning plagues or disease?

According to the *Oxford English Dictionary*, one definition of *pestilence* is "that which is morally pestilent or pernicious; moral plague or mischief, evil conduct, wickedness; that which is fatal to the public peace or well-being."[2]

If we will only trust Him, God is capable of saving us not only from deadly diseases but from those things that are morally corrupting as well.

Mark 12:31 quotes Jesus as saying, "Love your neighbor

as yourself." Philippians 2:3–4 tells us, "Do nothing out of selfish ambition or vain conceit. Rather, in humility value others above yourselves, not looking to your own interests but each of you to the interests of the others." And Jeremiah 29:7 is where Jeremiah tells the exiles in Babylon, "Also, seek the peace and prosperity of the city to which I have carried you into exile. Pray to the LORD for it, because if it prospers, you too will prosper."

If we disobey this command and do not seek the welfare of the city, the city suffers. We know we are to pray, but we also seek the city's welfare! That's the call to cultural engagement. Whether we are trying to feed the poor or serve in government, we are commanded to love our neighbor and seek the welfare of the city. A thriving city will benefit everyone. How can we seek its welfare if we are not involved with the governmental processes that determine that welfare? If you are called to serve in this way and you ignore that call, could it be that the fruit of that disobedience is what we are seeing running rampant throughout our world?

Christians are desperately needed in politics because if they are true, authentic Christians, they are people of integrity. They are called to have a higher standard than unbelievers, and they answer to someone other than just the voters.

> You are the salt of the earth. But if the salt loses its saltiness, how can it be made salty again? It is no longer good for anything, except to be thrown out and trampled underfoot by men. You are the light of the world. A town built on a hill cannot be hidden. Neither do people light a lamp and put it under a

> bowl. Instead they put it on its stand, and it gives
> light to everyone in the house. In the same way, let
> your light shine before others, that they may see
> your good deeds and glorify your Father in heaven.
> —Matthew 5:13–16

True Christians are salt and light. And the light shines best when it's dark! We are not perfect, but we know who we are and whose we are, and that is what makes us different. A true Christian is a follower of Christ. We are obedient to God's Word as well as sensitive to the Holy Spirit. We are led by the Spirit of God. If someone is truly following God and walking in obedience, that person will naturally have a higher level of integrity. Don't we need more people of integrity to serve in politics? That is why more Christians need to be involved.

Politics can be defined as the following: "the activities associated with the governance of a country or other area, especially the debate or conflict among individuals or parties having or hoping to achieve power"[3]; "the art or science of government; the art or science concerned with guiding or influencing governmental policy; [and] the art or science concerned with winning and holding control over a government."[4] If we are called to "rule and reign," if we are "more than conquerors," and we are to "seek the welfare of the city," how else can we do that if we are not involved in politics? John Dalberg-Acton, known as Lord Acton, once said, "Politics = the ethics of public life."[5]

In 1975, Loren Cunningham of Youth With a Mission and Bill Bright of Campus Crusade for Christ had a similar dream. They dreamed about seeing seven strategic mountains, or "mind molders," that influence and shape the culture of every nation. They believed that if they could transform each of these mountains they would transform the nations. Many others have written about this, and some have taken this original idea in directions that have caused controversy, which is unfortunate.

> *If we will only trust Him, God is capable of saving us not only from deadly diseases but from those things that are morally corrupting as well.*

I had the honor of getting to know Dr. Bright and his wife, Vonette, quite well before he died. To be clear, when I speak about the seven mountains concept, I am referring only to what Bright and Cunningham put forward.

In his book *Making Jesus Lord*, Cunningham writes:

> In 1975, I was praying and thinking about how we could turn the world around for Jesus. A list came to my mind: seven areas. We were to focus on these categories to turn around nations to God. I wrote them down, and stuck the paper in my pocket:
>
> 1. the home
>
> 2. the church
>
> 3. the schools
>
> 4. government and politics
>
> 5. the media
>
> 6. arts, entertainment and sports
>
> 7. commerce, science, and technology

The next day, I met with a dear brother, the leader of Campus Crusade for Christ, Dr. Bill Bright. He shared with me something God had given him— several areas to concentrate on to turn the nations back to God! They were the same areas, with different wording here and there, that were written on the page in my pocket. I took it out and showed Bill. Amazing coincidences like this happen all the time when Christians listen to the still, small voice of the Holy Spirit.

These seven spheres of influence will help us shape societies for Christ.[6]

So if we want to transform the mountain or sphere of government and are commanded as Christians to rule and reign, what does that mean?

Out of the seven mountains, many people consider the mountain of government and politics to be the most difficult. When Jesus was tempted in the wilderness, it wasn't the mountain of entertainment that Satan tried to tempt Him with three times. It wasn't the mountain of business. It was the mountain of government.

> Again, the devil took him to a very high mountain and showed him all the kingdoms of the world and their splendor. "All this I will give you," he said, "if you will bow down and worship me."
> —MATTHEW 4:8–9

Satan knows that the mountain of government influences all the rest. Perhaps that is why he has worked so hard to keep Christians out of it.

We all know that politics can be dangerous for the soul.

The temptations, pressures, and scrutiny can be enormous. But if you are called into that arena, God equips you to withstand all those things. So perhaps our nation, states, cities, counties, and school boards look as they do because we have allowed others to take the role we are supposed to have—a role that God has uniquely equipped us for over anyone else. By abdicating that role, perhaps we have allowed someone else, who is not equipped, to take it instead.

Moses questioned God's call on his life in Exodus 3:11: "Who am I that I should go to Pharaoh and bring the Israelites out of Egypt?" But God gives him what he needs to do the job He has asked him to do. How else will we get godly officials and leaders unless godly people run for office? Are we so lacking in faith that we believe God cannot handle the things that come up in politics? If David can defeat Goliath, and if God can split the Red Sea for the same Moses who doubted himself and at times probably questioned God, what can He do for you if you will merely step out in faith and trust Him?

CHAPTER 5

BUYING A SEAT IN CONGRESS

We have the best government that money can buy.
—AUTHOR UNKNOWN

DID YOU SEE the movie *The Devil Wears Prada*? In a profound scene, Miranda Priestly (Meryl Streep) educates Andy Sachs (Anne Hathaway) on how Andy chose the plain blue sweater she wore into the office that day.

Andy tells Miranda that she's still learning this fashion "stuff." And Miranda says: "This 'stuff'?" Miranda then clues Andy in on the fact that even though she doesn't think the fashion industry has anything to do with her, she is quite mistaken. She then decides to set her straight. Miranda says, "You go to your closet, and you select...that lumpy blue sweater...because you're trying to tell the world that you take yourself too seriously to care about what you put on your back. But what you don't know is that that sweater is not just blue, it's not turquoise, it's not lapis, it's actually cerulean."[1]

Andy learns that her clothing choice wasn't as random as she might have thought. Rather, it was part of a domino effect that started when one designer created a collection of gowns in that particular shade of blue, and then another designer launched a collection of military jackets in the same shade. As a result, eight other designers used

35

the same shade of blue in their collections, which is how she just *happened* to choose to wear a sweater that shade of blue. Miranda tells Andy, "That blue represents millions of dollars and countless jobs," and explains that it's sort of comical how Andy thinks she's made a choice that exempts her from the fashion industry when, in fact, she is wearing a sweater that was selected for her by the people in Miranda's office from a pile of "stuff."[2]

Now, you are probably wondering what a movie about fashion has to do with the current state of American politics. It's very simple. The candidate you think you chose in the last election was probably chosen for you. If you buy Kleenex at the store, grab an Uber to go downtown, or use Google as a verb, you are the successful target of branding. And often, the person you vote for is a human brand who has been chosen for you by a massive and very expensive team of experts who are driven by one thing: their paycheck.

According to LegBranch.org, "The 2000 election cycle, for example, saw House candidates spend a combined $2.9 billion on their campaigns. In 2016, that number exploded to $4.05 billion. [In the 2018] cycle, the average Representative raised $1.8 million for their reelection campaigns, up 80 percent from 2000."[3]

The American Bar Association offers this perspective: "In the past, the vehicles for political ads were newspapers, direct mail, radio, and television. In 2008, Barack Obama became one of the first candidates to use social media advertising in his campaign. That year, 2008, candidates spent a total of $22.25 million on online political ads.

Since then, online political advertising on [sic] has exploded—in 2016, candidates spent $1.4 billion on them."[4]

The 2022 elections are predicted to become the most expensive midterms in US history, with a record-breaking volume of TV, print, and digital ads.[5]

Here is the scariest fact of all, also from the American Bar Association: "Lying in political advertisements is also perfectly legal.... Why? Because political ads are considered political speech, and First Amendment law protects political speech above all other types of speech. The government has more leeway to penalize or censor commercial speech, but it has very little authority to regulate political ads."[6]

> *Having name recognition doesn't mean you're the best candidate, and it doesn't mean you're a good person. It may just mean that you have money to buy a lot of political advertising.*

The bottom line is not surprising to anyone; according to OpenSecrets, "The candidate who spends the most usually wins."[7]

Politics can be a racket—a treacherous, landmine-packed field. That atmosphere contributes heavily toward destroying the equality of who gets elected because money, not decisions focused on good government, is driving everything.

When I decided to run for office, I met with a member of Congress who commented, "Don't worry about the fact that you don't have name recognition. The truth is: you *buy* name recognition."

Having name recognition doesn't mean you're the best candidate, and it doesn't mean you're a good person. It may just mean that you have money to buy a lot of political advertising—but often voters don't think of it like that. They assume that if they see a certain person's name a lot, they must be the best candidate; sometimes, however, that is the furthest thing from the truth.

So guess what? If we want good people to win who cannot self-fund, we've got to get them some money! Most of the time, these candidates are not getting any money from the political action committees (PACs) or special interest groups that people typically donate to because many PACs don't get involved in primaries. So who do you give your money to and how? The next chapter will show you.

CHAPTER 6

DIPPING YOUR TOES INTO THE POND OF SUPPORT

Little things make a big difference.

—YOGI BERRA

GREATER POLITICAL ENGAGEMENT by people of faith can dramatically change a political landscape. And perhaps more corruption exists in certain states because of the lack of that very same type of involvement. For instance, Alabama ranks forty-seventh in the nation for political engagement, according to WalletHub,[1] and fourth highest in the nation for political corruption, according to the *Washington Post*.[2] Even more disturbing, Alabama is tied with Mississippi as *the* most religious state in the nation, with 77 percent of adults considering themselves to be "highly religious" and 82 percent of Alabama residents saying they believe in God with absolute certainty.[3] People of faith, we can do better!

The most recent Gallup Poll at the time of the publication of this book shows that 76 percent of Americans disapprove of Congress.[4] Americans lack trust in all levels of government, from their local city council members on up. We all know that bad actors are in the bunch, but you might be surprised to learn that there are honest, committed Christians *who are politicians too*! Honest candidates are running for office at every level of government, but we rarely see them because they often don't have as much money, so we rarely vote for them!

Sometimes it is hard to tell who the best candidates are, especially when they seem to all be saying the same things! So let's take first things first.

Good political engagement means voting. Every time. In every election! Next, it means that you as a voter must start treating elections more like job interviews instead of choosing candidates as you would a meal off of a fast-food menu. In many races, the ultimate decision is made in the primary (because the chances of someone winning from the other party in many districts is very unlikely), so it is *vital* to get involved in the primary races and the general election.

When I ran for Congress, seven candidates were in my race. On the surface, we sounded similar; but if you looked a little more closely, we couldn't have been more different.

So how do you tell the candidates apart? How do you separate the good from the mediocre and the bad? If you are merely looking at surface information, you will likely not be able to do it. Unfortunately, a lot of people spend more time researching which car to buy than which person to vote for. That is why, so often, they wind up being disappointed and throw their hands up at the whole process!

The key to changing this is to do your homework—for every candidate, at every level, in the primary and general elections. Let's face it, people vote for who they know. Many people will vote for the candidate they have heard of at the top of the ticket, and then as they move down the ballot and get to the names they don't know, they often don't vote.

Many people base who they will vote for on who has the most signs, the best TV ads, or the most billboards. In some cases, however, if you vote for the person with the most billboards, you may be voting for the person who is the least preferred candidate compared to the others!

The "halo effect bias" can be in full swing in politics. In other words, our view of the entire person can be based on one positive aspect, attractiveness being the most common. Good-looking people are frequently considered to

> *Unfortunately, a lot of people spend more time researching which car to buy than which person to vote for.*

be of higher moral caliber. Or perhaps if one candidate is filmed attending church, that positive image will be used to judge the rest of his actions.

If you are a busy mom or someone who can't devote a lot of time and energy to politics, then find others you trust who have studied each candidate. Find someone who can steer you in the right direction by giving you information to make an informed decision. One of the great things about being a Christian is having others in the body of Christ you can seek out for help.

In his book *The Tipping Point,* Malcolm Gladwell describes three types of people: Connectors, Mavens, and Salesmen. I have a neighborhood friend named Julie, who is a maven. A maven is defined as "someone experienced or knowledgeable."[5] This person is an expert with vast information stores.

Julie eats, sleeps, and breathes politics. She is a strong Christian and has been tracking state, local, and national politics for years. When I haven't made up my mind about who the best city council member candidate or congressional candidate is, I call Julie and ask, "Who do you like who is running for this office, and why?" I do this because I know Julie has researched these things, and she and I have the same values. I have found that no matter where I've lived, others like Julie are happy to share their research with me. The sharing of research is another sign of a maven.

I also call my friend David, who tracks issues in my home state and nationally. I trust David and know he is in the thick of things with all of the issues going on right now. So I might call him and say, "OK, I'm in between these issues and policy decisions, or these candidates. What can you tell me about them?" He will then give me all sorts of resources and education so I can decide based on facts.

Afterward, I compare what Julie and David have told me with what others I know who are well-informed and like-minded are saying. I take all that information, pray about my decision, and then get involved.

If you can't find a Julie or a David in your neighborhood or community, get involved in some of the national organizations that share your values. You will most likely meet people in your state or hometown who are highly informed about politics at all levels. They can help guide you to good people who can give you the right information so that you too can make an informed decision when you vote.

Suppose you have worked hard to know who is running for office in your community or state. You've done your homework and chosen a candidate you can get behind, knowing that genuine support means more than just casting your vote on Election Day and sending up your prayers. Let's examine the variety of ways you can provide meaningful help to your candidate.

Start with getting to know your candidate online. Likely, every candidate has a website that includes their biography and platform. You will find details about their experience, family, education, community involvement, and career. If you unearth very few details about their life before candidacy, let that be a warning bell. Dig deeper.

Next, follow your candidate's social media platforms. Generally, Facebook, Twitter, and Instagram will provide updates on issues and events faster and more comprehensively than a website. Want to know how a candidate is responding to a major news event? Check their posts to keep track of their statements. Social media accounts will also advertise your candidate's public appearances. Watch the videos they post. Do they use gimmicks and rhetoric to get your attention, or are they speaking from the heart and showing that they have substance and true values? Do their past actions match up with what they are saying? Most importantly, pull up their financial disclosure forms, and pay attention to who is donating to their campaign. OpenSecrets.org is a good place to start to find out if they are taking money from people or corporations that do not align with your values.

Most importantly, meet your candidate! According to the MIT Election Data and Science Lab, in any given election, between 35 percent and 60 percent of eligible voters don't cast a ballot.[6] The majority of voters are Christian,[7] but many eligible Christians don't turn out to vote. According to the Family Research Council, "We cannot win the public debate over the critical issues of faith, family, and freedom if like-minded Americans stay home on Election Day."[8]

MIT's election lab has also determined this: "When it comes to local elections, overall turnout rates tend to be much lower than elections held to coincide with federal elections, and the demographic characteristics of voters are much more skewed than compared to non-voters."[9] This is disturbing because many decisions are made on the local level, impacting things like election integrity, education policies, and zoning issues.

It is also important to attend local events where your candidate is scheduled to appear. Invite your friends to go with you, even those who have not decided which candidate they will throw their support behind. These grassroots events are often held in church halls and coffee shops. The crowds are smaller in these locations, making it easier to meet your candidate one on one.

Attending a town hall event will allow you to put a question to your candidate and listen to how he or she handles difficult questions from other voters. Do they remain calm and polite, or do they dodge and weave or flare up with annoyance? How patient is your candidate when they respond? They will be asked the same questions repeatedly throughout their campaign, which means they should be prepared and patient. You have an opportunity to watch your candidate respond to opposition and judge for yourself how they function under pressure. How they act during campaign events and public appearances can indicate how they will deal with their constituency and staff once elected.

Not only are you learning about your candidate, but your presence at their events bolsters their optimism, encourages them to keep going, and gets media attention by increasing crowd size.

So drop in at your candidate's campaign headquarters; the public is welcome at these locations. Meet the staff and others in your community who are supporting your candidate. Doing so will give you insight into the campaign's needs and ways you can be of support. If you like what you see, there will be volunteer opportunities, like making phone calls or putting up signs, with a commitment of as little as an hour or two a week.

These are the typical things that most people think to do. But what if your candidate doesn't have a campaign headquarters? What does that mean? The candidate who has the most money and can afford a big fancy headquarters and billboards on every corner may not be the one who has your best interests at heart.

Sometimes the best candidate has very little money because they are not independently wealthy and refuse to take money from groups that will want to own them after they get elected. That means they are also the ones who may not have anywhere near as much purchased visibility. Quite possibly what they do have is exactly the right experience, heart, and passion for serving their community. They may be a populist candidate, not a self-serving politician.

CHAPTER 7

LESS THAN 1 PERCENT

The price of greatness is responsibility.
—Winston Churchill

B UT HOW, YOU may ask, do Christians support the candidates who carry Christian values to the statehouse, the Senate, Congress, or the White House? Mostly, they don't.

According to OpenSecrets, in 2016, the percentage of Americans who gave more than $200 to political campaigns *was less than 1 percent.*[1]

In 2020, even as strongly as many people on both sides felt about the elections, that number only jumped up to 1.44 percent of the US population that contributed more than $200 to federal candidates, PACs, parties, and outside groups.[2] So only a tiny fraction of the American population was involved in a way that put skin in the game!

If so few people are donating to political campaigns, is it any wonder that our political leaders have forgotten about the people's interests? As I've stated, political campaigns take money. With 70 percent of US citizens identifying as Christians,[3] how does this translate to the number of Christians who donate? Answer: a microscopic few. Is it any wonder then that we have been electing the kind of leaders we have?

According to Giving USA, Americans donated $471 billion to private charities in 2020,[4] and the number of private foundations more than doubled from 1995 to 2017.[5] But where most Christians fail to make the connection is that this level of support is equally important in the political arena. If you don't like the laws that you see passed, you must support the candidates who represent your values. That means voting with your wallet! We need to ask why it is easier for Christians to give money to foreign aid organizations than to the potential political leaders in our own country who make the decisions that literally impact *everything* we do.

Do we feel better about ourselves when we give to those poor foreign babies because we see pictures of their swollen bellies and sad eyes and it pulls on our heartstrings?

I am certainly not suggesting that we stop helping children in need. I have spent a large portion of my career trying to do just that. But I believe that just as it is important to help starving children, we also need to think about the leaders who make the decisions that impact our lives every day. These decisions influence our laws, our livelihoods, and the quality of our lives. If we elect better leaders, maybe we won't have so many starving children.

One political consultant explained to me that for the liberal Left, politics *is* their religion, and they tithe to it on a regular basis. They have no problem writing checks, even if they're small checks, because they understand that many little checks can add up to way more than a few big ones.

To transform our government into something in line with God's will, we must rise up and engage on this level as the body of Christ. And no, this is not going to replace a tithe.

There is only one place where tithes should go and that is to the church. The church is the place that feeds you spiritually.

In addition to tithing, we must recognize that there are things we invest in that affect our future. Good government impacts everything and is no different from any other investment. We have no problem investing in stocks. We have no problem investing in insurance to protect our house if it catches on fire. We have no problem investing in sports teams to build them into champions. We invest in a multitude of things, but for some reason, we've drawn a line with political candidates. Now is the time to change that.

> *For the liberal Left, politics is their religion, and they tithe to it on a regular basis.*

Presume you have given your candidate your verbal backing, and now it is time to contribute your financial backing.

To a candidate, every dollar counts. With the massive campaign budgets required to send a candidate to Washington, you may think that candidates are only interested in million-dollar donors. Many Christians have given up and don't think they can make a difference because of the vast amount of money that pours into politics from special interest groups. But that is simply not true. Crowdfunding—gathering small amounts of money from large groups of people—is shifting this dynamic.

In the film *Finding Nemo*, Nemo, a clownfish, and his dad, Marlin, watch in horror as a school of larger fish is hauled into a boat toward a most certain demise. Nemo and Marlin begin to yell to the other fish, "Swim down together!" As they do, the little fish find that if they work together, they can break the net that has captured them and swim to freedom. While rather simplistic, this scene reminds me of what we can do in political environments as well. You may think that your $25 donation given directly to a good candidate may not mean much, but collectively, if you along with enough of your friends and neighbors give, it starts to add up. Think about how many small businesses get started with crowdsourcing apps like Kickstarter!

To maintain its 501(c)(3) status as a nonprofit organization, your church cannot financially support candidates; therefore, you as an individual must actively support candidates who have Christian values.

The days of getting out the checkbook, penning a check, addressing an envelope, finding a stamp, and licking the envelope are over. Within seconds (ninety on average), more than a billion people worldwide are making donations by text, and the donation amount (on average $100) is added to their cell phone bill.

In the last presidential election, estimates were as high as thirteen billion for the total number of campaign texts sent.[6] Political SMS marketing firm Tatango claims they can send seven million donation messages an hour.[7]

In other words, making donating easier has increased small donor participation in political campaigns. "For example, the Bernie Sanders campaign attracted 1.3 million small donations (from 650,000 individual donors)."[8]

Tatango also reveals that 78 percent of Rep. Alexandria Ocasio-Cortez's (D-NY) 2020 funding was derived from *small donors.*[9]

According to marketplace.org, small-dollar political

donations reach the two-billion-dollar mark, or roughly 24 percent of political giving.[10] Your donation *does* make a difference. You can make an impact at any giving level. But it can also be very confusing during election season when you may be bombarded with requests to know how to give in the best way.

CHAPTER 8

THE RISE OF THE SUPER PAC

When solving problems, dig at the roots
instead of just hacking at the leaves.
—ANTHONY J. D'ANGELO

FRIEND OF MINE in Pennsylvania recently sent me this message: "I get all these emails from different senators, governors, and people running for office. And it's not just for candidates; it's fighting this or fighting that. One of them wants me to sign a petition, but then they want a donation to go along with that. How does it work with all these different people? Do I just contribute directly to a PAC and let them get the money to the seats that need it most? How in the world would I know if I am being scammed sending it to any of these individuals?"

My friend presents a very good question. So let's start at the beginning to give a brief history of how we got to where we are right now with political fundraising. When you are a declared candidate for federal office, the maximum amount you can receive from an individual for your campaign is $2,900 per election. If a donor wants to give more than that, their only legal mechanism to do so is through a PAC. There are also statewide PACs for use only in state races and that are governed by each state's election laws.

There are five types of federal PACs. A regular, or

"connected," PAC is "a political committee established and administered by corporations, labor unions, membership organizations and trade associations. The general definition is a group that spends money on elections, but is not run by a party or individual candidate."[1] A multicandidate PAC can donate up to $5,000 directly to state and local parties or candidates they support and up to $15,000 to a national party committee. An example of this would be a PAC set up by a company like AT&T or an organization like the American Federation of Teachers. There are also hybrid PACs (also known as a Carey committee, which can maintain two separate accounts) and leadership PACs (which are controlled by a candidate or federal officeholder).

Then there are super PACs (like the one that approached my friend). These PACs came into existence in July 2010 following two key federal court decisions. A federal super PAC is formed primarily to make "independent expenditures" in support or opposition of a federal candidate. "An independent expenditure is a communication, such as a website, newspaper, TV, or direct mail advertisement that: expressly advocates the success or defeat of a clearly identified candidate for federal office; and is not made in consultation or cooperation with, or at the request or suggestion of any candidate, or his or her authorized committees or agents, or a political party committee or its agents."[2]

These types of PACs "can accept unlimited contributions and spend an unlimited amount supporting or opposing federal election candidates."[3] Still, they cannot directly donate to federal candidates or parties. "The role of a super PAC is similar to that of a traditional political action committee. A super PAC advocates for the election or defeat of candidates for federal office by purchasing television, radio, and print advertisements as well as other forms of media marketing. There are conservative super PACs and liberal super PACs."[4]

Super PACs can be a powerful force in electing candidates if used correctly, and many of them do a lot of good. They can help level the playing field if a candidate is outspent by an opponent. Supporters of a candidate can form a PAC, and there is then no limit on donations that can be received to support them.

Because it is very hard to raise a lot of funds for a campaign quickly with a $2,900 cap per individual donor, according to Federal Election Commission (FEC) regulations, a super PAC can be set up to benefit a federal candidate and raise large amounts of money fast. Often, this is needed if a seat suddenly becomes open and there is very little time to plan fundraisers and reach out to a lot of donors. PACs also work to inform voters and to equip them with the information they may find useful before casting their votes.

With the growing decline of investigative journalism in America due to newspapers' financial struggles, super PACs are now, in some ways, also filling "the role" of journalists. Often, they draw attention to certain issues that a candidate may not want to point out themselves because of the public distaste for negative campaigning by candidates directly.

According to *Harvard Magazine*, "Since Congress passed a 'Stand by Your Ad' provision in 2002, candidates have been required to give the now-familiar 'I endorse this message' at the end of all commercials sponsored directly by their campaigns; and when these advertisements go very negative, there's a real risk of a backlash that does more harm than good. But commercials sponsored by independent organizations, and aired without a candidate's endorsement, sidestep this problem. More significantly, voters also tend to believe them more, according to psychological studies.

"Campaign managers appear to understand this phenomenon very well: [in the 2016 primary races,] 88 percent of official, campaign-sponsored advertisements in Iowa and New Hampshire were positive, compared with just 35 percent of super PAC ads."[5]

However, because this is a relatively new political industry, it is still, in essence, the Wild West! More and more of these types of PACs are being set up every day, and as with every industry, there are some good actors and some bad. Unfortunately, the rise of scam PACs is becoming more prevalent, and there is no "Good Housekeeping Seal of Approval" to make sure that you are dealing with a legitimate group.[6]

If you are, for example, a typical middle-class person who understands the need to give but wants to do it the right way, what are you to do? If you don't know the right way to give and the right questions to ask as a donor, a large portion of your money may end up in the pocket of some overpaid consultant or vendor. The Center for Public Integrity has some shocking statistics about super PAC spending in 2013:

- "Fewer than one in seven of the roughly 300 super PACs and 'hybrid' PACs that spent money in 2013 put funds toward calling for the election or defeat of a federal candidate."

- "Less than a sixth of the $109 million spent by super PACs and hybrid PACS...went to independent efforts to support or oppose federal candidates."

- "Almost half of the groups' itemized reported expenses...went toward overhead costs such as salaries, payments to consultants, and marketing."

- With one super PAC in particular, "two-thirds of expenses went to consultants. The average super PAC spent about a quarter of its cash on consultants and compensation in 2013."[7]

Rick Hasen, a law and political science professor at the University of California, Irvine, who publishes the *Election Law Blog*, said, "Super PACs are not just about influencing elections—they are a source of income for political consultants."[8]

Sheila Krumholz, who tracks political spending at the Center for Responsive Politics, said in 2014, "Right now, there are 109 super PACs in our data that reported spending money but have made no independent expenditures." All they are doing, Krumholz said, is paying staff and consultants to help them raise more money. "They are capitalizing on political interests in order to siphon off money that would otherwise go to support candidates and parties, and instead, they are using it for their own personal enrichment."[9]

Each election cycle, the cost of running for office just

keeps going up and up. Trevor Potter, former chair of the FEC, said, during the same podcast in which Krumholz was interviewed, that consulting for super PACs is "the new growth industry." According to the Brennan Center for Justice, "The apex for super PACs so far has been 2016, when they poured over $1 billion into federal elections, accounting for 16 percent of all spending."[10] As of June 4, 2022, 2,163 groups organized as super PACs have reported total receipts of $1,130,917,179 and total independent expenditures of $235,021,530 in the 2021–2022 cycle.[11]

Our process for democracy has been turned into a for-profit industry, and it keeps accelerating like a nuclear arms race. The only way to stop this? Put honest people in office who will vote to reform the system. Those benefiting from the system will never do this, so we must elect leaders who will support campaign finance reform and allow themselves to be held accountable. Meanwhile, this is the system we must work within if we are truly going to bring about change.

Having run a super PAC and worked on multiple campaigns at all levels of government, I had to be schooled myself about the pitfalls in this business. Speaking as someone who has worked around or been involved with politics my entire adult life, I thought I knew a lot about how things are supposed to work. Here are three points I picked up quickly:

1. As I explained previously, although some legitimate super PACs exist, some are fly-by-night organizations and in the wrong hands

can almost be a license to steal with very little oversight or accountability.

2. When giving to a super PAC, you must be very discerning. Most PACs are run by consultants, and they usually take a salary. Fundraisers also take a cut—either as a salary or a percentage of how much they raise. Next, the money in the PAC is used to hire vendors, and the vendors all take a cut. Lawyers, media buyers, and others are also paid out of the PAC. In my experience, most honest vendors take a 15 percent profit margin on any work they do for a PAC. However, if the people running the PAC are not honest, kickbacks, excessive fees, and high salaries may be a large percentage of what your donated money goes to fund. Salaries for those running super PACs can be in the six- or seven-figure range, with return on investment being as low as 14 percent.[12] There also is no legal limit on what a fundraiser can be paid at the state or federal level.

3. There are a lot of ways to hide what happens to the money. Money that comes into a super PAC is subject to federal reporting requirements. But once the money from the PAC is transferred to a vendor or consultant, that is where the information often stops. The expenditure report for the PAC may only list the vendor's name, the purpose of

the expense, and nothing more. If a PAC is not above board, those running the PAC can take your money, transfer it to a vendor, and then have the vendor give them a huge kickback just for sending them the business. Due to the time-sensitive nature of campaigns, there often is very little time to vet things the way a normal consumer would, and quite often what shows up on expenditure reports makes it very hard to tell how the money was spent.

Vendors to the PAC are not required by FEC laws to give a reporting to anyone. Because the vendor is a private entity, exact information on how it spent the money it was paid could only be obtained if fraud were suspected and legal action were taken. So a vendor could keep most of the money it received to do a job or service, and there would be little way to know unless the PAC requires actual receipts for services performed. Due to the time-sensitive nature of campaigns, there often is very little time to vet things the way a normal consumer would, and quite often what shows up on expenditure reports makes it very hard to tell how the money was spent. These are the types of things that you as the donor may never discover if you are dealing with a dishonest PAC.

Often, it is *very* confusing to people who are new or uninformed to distinguish between a legitimate super PAC and a scam PAC. Also, some fundraising organizations are set up to do only one thing for the candidate: give them your name as a donor. If you give to one of these organizations, they typically keep the majority of the money as their fee for finding you and turning over your name. If you fall prey to

> *Our process for democracy has been turned into a for-profit industry, and it keeps accelerating like a nuclear arms race.*

one of these operations, the candidate usually doesn't get much money from your first donation. Not until you give again, after the candidate contacts you directly, does the candidate receive the bulk of your monetary contribution.

One fundraiser friend working with a federal campaign recently told me that her candidate received a $500 donation from a donor. She said to me, "Guess how much the fundraising company sent the candidate out of that $500?" The answer: $1. The company kept $499 of the donation just to give the candidate the donor's name. This happens because, quite often, elected officials are way too busy to go out and find good donors. So they rely on others who provide services to do this, many unscrupulously. This will only stop if donors get a whole lot smarter.

In my research for this book, it has also become evident that a growing concern regarding campaign finance needs to be addressed. The entire political action committee space, from the original PACs to what are now known as super PACs, is, in many ways, an industry that can breed corruption on both sides of the political aisle if not carefully kept in check. As reforms are being discussed regarding insider trading for our elected officials, this too needs investigation and congressional action.

For people of conscience and faith, now is the moment that your engagement truly may change the world. If you don't get involved, the tipping point could be in the other direction, and our country may have to endure years of darkness. This book aims to motivate people to engage in the political process as a mission and a cultural change endeavor to turn the nation back to its founding principles.

Please understand that I am pointing out some negative aspects of political giving *not* to discourage you from being a donor but to do the exact opposite. Because money often drives everything, your donations are needed now more than ever. Still, you need to be a *smart* donor and make sure you contribute to the solution, not further contribute to the problem! Whether we like it or not, super PACs are likely here to stay and have become a dominant force in US elections, *so we must learn to "fight fire with fire,"* so to speak.

Money follows vision, and money needs to be part of stewardship. My friend and colleague Frank Wright, PhD, former president of Coral Ridge Ministries, often says, "You can tell everything you really need to know about where someone is in their walk with Christ by looking at two things, their checkbook and their datebook. Where do they spend their time, and where do they spend their money?"[13]

The only way to fight the money that governs today's politics is with money and greater personal engagement. A political campaign is ultimately a branding and marketing campaign with a human brand. If you are launching a new product, you need a marketing budget. So what is the best way to give and avoid some of the pitfalls I just outlined?

First and foremost, before you give anywhere else, donate to the candidate's campaign directly. If you can give more than the $2,900 federal limit, please see my next chapter, which is specifically for major donors. But if all you have to give is $100, give it to the candidate! Make sure you are giving it directly to the candidate, *not to an organization claiming to fundraise on behalf of the candidate!*

Go to their campaign website. Make sure it says, "Paid for by John Doe for Governor" or "Paid for by Jane Smith for Senate" on the bottom of the page, and give to them there, or better yet, go to a campaign event and hand them a check directly so they can save the credit card fee! By doing this, you go straight to the source and your donation will do the most good.

It is also important to understand that incumbents have an advantage over challengers. The incumbent knows the system, the players, and donors and usually has money left in the bank from previous campaigns. Incumbents in the US House of Representatives, for example, are re-elected almost 90 percent of the time![14] Even if the incumbent is doing a terrible job and needs to be voted out of office, a challenger will overcome the odds only if voters back them solidly and show their support financially. Incumbents and challengers need to raise money to fund their campaigns so they can spend the money on mailers, yard signs, bumper stickers, social media, and TV and radio ads. They also have to hire campaign consultants, compliance experts, lawyers, and fundraisers.

Crowdfunding from small donors opens up the political

field to qualified, caring citizens who would have otherwise faced an economic barrier to throwing their hats in the ring. Your monetary support plays an important role in supporting Christian candidates who share your values in more than just what they say but also in what they do.

Fundraising from a larger donor base that is reached from crowdfunding initiatives improves the chances of candidates who could not otherwise afford to run—because what you give money to, you care about. Even if it's only $25, that gift can mean a lot to a candidate because it shows you are committed to them.

CHAPTER 9

HOW TO BE A SMART DONOR

What you feed lives; what you starve dies.
—Author Unknown

WHILE HAVING LUNCH with a friend who sold his company for more than $70 million, I asked what he seeks to accomplish when he gives to political causes. He gave me the usual answers: "I want to help elect good leaders and make an impact in the upcoming elections, etc."

I then asked him, "How do you ensure that the money you give is actually used in the way you intend it to be?" He sheepishly answered that he just doesn't understand politics that much—that it isn't a business he has ever been in and that he just has to trust that the people he gives to are doing the right thing. I have heard this answer over and over.

And therein lies the problem.

Most businesspeople have made their money because they're smart, and for the most part, they have a high degree of discernment. But when it comes to politics, a lot of people think, *I'm really good at business; therefore, I will be good at politics.* Unfortunately, quite often, that is the furthest thing from the truth.

Most wealthy people being asked to give money to politics have never been in politics. Some of them truly don't understand the process enough to ensure that the organization they are giving to is effective and managed with integrity.

So if you, Mr. Christian millionaire, really are trying for all the right reasons to help the country and want to give, for example, $100,000 to help good candidates get elected—how are you going to give that money to be most effective? Your success allows you to share your abundance to better your brothers and sisters in Christ. But you also need to invest those gifts wisely.

In my work with major donors all over the country, some have told me that they are often made to feel like they just need to let those "in the know" make the decisions. They feel like there is often little or no effort made to truly empower or educate them about what they are actually funding. Because of the time-sensitive nature of political campaigns, it has been very easy for self-serving individuals to take advantage of those writing the checks. We must stop letting the tail wag the dog and encourage more donors to take control.

As a major donor, you have a right to ask the hard questions up front and to choose wisely. Better yet, if you have significant resources, you should consider forming your own super PAC or state-level PAC! Doing this will cut out *a lot* of middlemen, and you can influence the specific races you want to impact.

If you decide to set up a PAC, you will most likely need to hire someone to run it for you. Finding someone who has integrity and is aligned with your values and is extremely politically savvy will be necessary. Making sure you hire a person who has both business and political knowledge is very important because a large percentage of the vendors in the political space will most likely not share your values.

Not all, but many of them are only in it for the money and don't care if a candidate wins as long as they get paid. It is critical to have someone working with the PAC who can identify good vendors and knows how to negotiate with them. *By setting up your own PAC, you control where the money goes and ensure that the bulk of it goes directly to independent expenditures*

> As a major donor, you have a right to ask the hard questions up front and to choose wisely.

through honest vendors. You also can be certain that the money will be targeted to the right kinds of candidates only.

Many first-time candidates for federal office don't even understand the need for having a super PAC support them when they are new to the process. So if you want to be effective, recruit top-notch candidates to run, and get behind them fully with the backing and support they need. This is what happens with many of the "establishment" candidates. They are recruited and preselected because they will play ball with the powers that be; then they are backed by those entities and their super PACs or PACs once they enter the arena. This ensures that only candidates who they in essence "own" will be elected. The *only* way to combat this? High-net-worth individuals with integrity must come together and fully back candidates looking to serve because they are called and trained.

The emergence of the super PAC marked the start of a new era in politics. Today, most elections are determined largely by how much money is flowing into them. This has resulted in more power being placed into the hands of the wealthy. Few would agree that democracy should only reflect the views of the affluent. If you are a wealthy, committed Christian, could it be that God has blessed you with your wealth so that you may overcome the agenda of those who are not using their resources for good?

Billions of dollars are being poured into our country right now to fund movements and legislation that are ultimately designed to destroy the fabric of the United States and undermine Christian values. Who else can counteract the efforts of people like George Soros and others but those who are also of significant means who come together and push back against their efforts?

As previously stated, if you are a Christian millionaire (or billionaire), you can make an enormous difference by setting up your own super PAC; or you can form one jointly with other wealthy individuals whom you know and trust. By establishing a political action committee, you can avoid a lot of the shenanigans that happen with money that funds organizations you have no control over and that have little to no transparency. If every high-net-worth Christian in the United States did this, that one thing could make a significant impact on our elections alone. Most importantly, by giving your money to people who are vetted and not just giving it to organizations, you target your money directly into the place it most needs to go, and you can be a great help to those who are running for office.

Another critical point is that we must change our approach to *when* we get involved. One of the greatest problems many good, honest candidates face is getting through a primary. Most large super PACs do not get involved in primary races. But typically, the primaries are where you weed out the real, called candidates from the rest. As author and direct mail guru Richard Viguerie puts it, "It's the primaries, stupid."[1] Often, voters are not paying attention to primaries, and that is how a lot of Christians in name only slip through and wind up getting elected. Once they are in office, their voting record does not match up to what they promised when campaigning, but by then, it's too late!

In many races, the true outcome is decided in the primary. In a lot of districts or precincts, the majority of voters are registered to one party, so the general election is more of a formality; the real winner has already been determined in the primaries. This makes primary races even more critical, but most people don't pay much attention to them. In Texas, for example, according to the Texas Tribune, "Voter participation in midterm primary elections is dismal…, with less than a quarter of registered voters casting ballots most years. This means that a vast majority of registered voters don't participate."[2] Again, the only way to change this is for more major donors to get involved, not just in the general election but in the primaries!

Also, many large donors prefer to get involved in national politics instead of state or local politics. They are lured by the fun, exciting dinners and photo ops that national political events offer that local events often don't.

However, the impact of your donation on a state or local level can be enormously powerful, and it typically takes far less money to influence these types of races.

"For down-ticket races, it stands to reason that political

advertising effects are even *stronger* than for the presidential race," *Harvard Magazine* reported. "Even the most hardened politicos do not generally discuss the local state legislative race at the dinner table."[3] But perhaps they should.

Advertising and local media coverage constitute a larger percentage of the information diet for the less publicized races, giving them greater importance, especially now that these races so often reflect presidential-style campaigning. [4]

As a steward of significant resources, you need to get involved in a strategic way. Major donors must understand the need to not only give, but to give smarter. To paraphrase Jesus' words in Luke 12:48, to whom much is given, much is required.

Below are some things to consider as a major donor:

1. Pray first. Ask God to show you who you should support with the money you have been blessed with and trusted to steward.

2. Consider establishing your own super PAC or state-level PAC.

3. Ask hard questions. You will find a list of questions in this chapter that you should consider asking when someone approaches you to donate.

4. Give early. Early money can make a big difference, especially in a primary race where the candidate is trying to gain momentum.

5. Give a test gift. Watch how that is handled. If it is managed well, then give more.

6. Hold fundraisers at your home for a candidate and invite your friends. This can make a huge difference for a new candidate. Don't just give. Get involved.

7. Be proactive with your money and recruit good candidates. Get together with other high-net-worth individuals and nominate people of high integrity in your community, city, district, or state to run. Then get behind them financially, and encourage those in your networks to do the same.

8. Understand the pressures. If your candidate is a member of Congress, they have a constant requirement to fundraise. The minute they are elected, they have to start thinking about being re-elected and getting a committee assignment. The practice of members of Congress having to "pay" or fundraise a certain amount each year to get a committee assignment needs to be stopped; but unfortunately, right now, until we put pressure on Congress and elect those who will change those practices, that is the system under which most members of Congress must operate. Committee assignments used to be given based upon merit, knowledge of issues, and the needs of a member's district. That has all changed. If you are someone who is not looking for anything from them other than good government and wise leadership,

you can help take some of this pressure off
by contributing to them financially and
fundraising for them in between elections so
they can focus on doing the job they were
sent there to do.

9. Give money *directly*. Remember that the
   most effective thing you can do is give
   money directly to the candidate first.

10. Support your candidate through a PAC.
    Once you've given the maximum amount
    allowed by law to the campaign directly, con-
    sider giving to a super PAC supporting that
    candidate if you can give more. If a super
    PAC is not backing the candidate, consider
    setting one up yourself to support them.

As a former congressional candidate, I can tell you that
the money that came in early in my race meant everything. When a candidate announces that they are running
for office, the first thing most people in the political world
do is look at how much money they have raised. If, right
off the bat, the candidate can issue a press release saying
that they have raised $200,000, for example, this accom-
plishes two things.

First, it shows that they are a serious, viable candidate
with major donor support, which makes other donors want
to give to them. Key organizations are also more likely to
endorse them. Second, it keeps other candidates from getting in the race because they will see that the other person
has gained a strong lead. It can also give a candidate an

advantage in buying TV airtime. The earlier they buy, the better the price and the better the time slots. It is more expensive for a PAC to buy airtime than for a candidate to buy it through their campaign; that is another reason to give the money directly to the candidate first. In addition, super PACs can pay up to six times as much to run TV ads as actual campaigns, so a donation to the campaign can make your money go further.[5]

According to Mentzer Media, "Candidates and their official campaign entities are entitled by federal law to the 'lowest unit rate' on TV, cable and radio within 45 days of a Primary election, and 60 days prior to a General election....Issue advertisers and Super PACs receive no such rate protection or guarantee of access—and are often charged exorbitant rates by media outlets."[6] To put it simply, super PACs must spend two million to three million dollars to have the advertising impact an official campaign could purchase for one million dollars.

Running a campaign is like starting a business. When someone is deciding whether to run for office, they need backers, just as small business startups need seed money.

When I prayed about running for Congress and felt very clearly that I was supposed to run, I immediately started praying next about who to go to for support. I felt prompted to call a friend who knows me well, is a strong Christian, and is a person of significant means. I told her what I was feeling led to do.

She asked me several questions and said, "Terri, I want to support you and donate to your campaign, and I will ask others to also. If you decide to run, I will get behind you 100 percent." It meant so much to know that she believed in me, and it was also a confirmation that I was going in the right direction. But most importantly, it emboldened me to move forward and take the first steps to file the paperwork and hire a team because I knew I had the backing I needed. I'm quite certain that other people of faith feel called and would probably be braver to step out and run for office if they had someone like my friend to support them. You could be that someone.

If you give to a candidate's campaign and they lose the election, you have not lost your investment. There must be a paradigm shift to keep in mind that you are investing in the person more than the race or office. This is the spiritual view.

I knew God called me to run. I didn't know if He called me to win. Because I ran, that experience trained me. I learned a great deal, and the result is this book. I have also gained the knowledge I will take into the next race, and I share that knowledge to help other candidates. So if you donated to my last race, you didn't lose your investment. Your investment may impact many people, but we forget this and feel like our money is wasted if our candidate loses.

Anyone who invests money expects a return. Apple's IPO in 1980 was $22 a share. By the end of 2004, its stock price had climbed to $64.40,[7] and in 2021, shares reached a high of $182.94.[8] We're all looking for steady, healthy growth. When we invest in a candidate, we are investing in the future of our country and need to be in it for the long haul.

Think of your political contribution as investing in a startup. When Apple went public in 1980 at $22 a share, you would not have expected Apple stock to hit $50 the next day. No, you had faith. You waited and watched. And your $1,000 investment in 1980 would have been worth $430,000 in 2018.[9]

As stewards of great resources, donors must learn to invest their gifts wisely when it comes to the political arena. The abundance given to you through grace should not be tossed around like confetti, nor should it be withheld from what is truly one of the most vital places Christians are needed. You have a sacred trust to share your abundance and all that is given to you with prudence and discernment.

In summary, first and foremost you should always give to the candidate's campaign directly. After you have done that, the most effective and efficient way to use your money if you are a major donor and you will be giving a large donation is to set up your own super PAC or state-level PAC. If you do not want to do that, then ask the candidate if they have a PAC they would like to direct you toward.

As a general rule, always ask some questions before writing a big check to a PAC.

Here are examples of things you may want to ask:

- What kinds of salaries are paid by the PAC, and how many full-time employees and consultants do you have?

- What are your administrative costs? (Anything higher than 15 percent should be a red flag.)

- What portion of the budget is going toward independent expenditures such as TV/radio, digital advertising, etc.? (This should be where the bulk of the money is focused.)

- Do any of your vendors have a personal relationship with the consultants or staff running the PAC?

- Do you put projects out for bid?

- Do you require your vendors to provide a draft of what is being produced and analytics reports (if it was distributed online)? Will you show me receipts or give me a return-on-investment report so I can see how my money has been spent?

- Will my money be used for a TV commercial? If so, can I see it before it runs? (Make sure they are running a quality commercial. Sometimes the ads are executed so poorly that they do more harm than good. Ask to see the ad first!)

These are things you just do not know until you are in it with your hip waders. My experience running for office and running a super PAC forced me to learn to ask these questions. When my donors invested in my campaign, they invested in this kind of education. It is an education I am now sharing with you and those who are looking to run for political office.

So keep the faith; after all, in 1990, Apple closed the year at 31 cents per share.

CHAPTER 10

IF YOU ARE CALLED

It is important for you to understand that when God calls you to something, He is not always calling you to succeed, He is calling you to obey! The obedience to the call is up to you—the success of the call is up to Him!
—GARY WILKERSON

RUDYARD KIPLING'S MOST famous poem was written for his only son, John, and is known simply as "If." Even though it was meant as a way for a father to impart wisdom to his son, it is also a poem that has great application in the sphere of politics. It reminds me of what sets a statesman apart from a politician. In "If," Kipling writes:

> If you can keep your head when all about you
> Are losing theirs and blaming it on you,
> If you can trust yourself when all men doubt you,
> But make allowance for their doubting too;
> If you can wait and not be tired by waiting,
> Or being lied about, don't deal in lies,
> Or being hated, don't give way to hating...[1]

What would politics look like if people who are called to serve fully responded to that call? And as Christians, if we choose to serve, shouldn't we be different from those who don't know Christ? In addition to demonstrating integrity, staying humble, and adhering to Christian values, there is one thing more that truly sets us apart: the ability to not give in to hate.

Indeed, it is perhaps only by God's grace and His Spirit that anyone could tolerate being hated without giving in to hate in return or being lied about and not themselves wanting to seek revenge or deal in lies. True Christians have the power of the Holy Spirit,

What would politics look like if people who are called to serve fully responded to that call?

which grants them the ability to overcome the natural desires of the flesh, including the desire to lie or hate. This is all the more reason they are needed in politics now more than ever, because isn't the world full of enough hate already? God has given us the power to overcome hate, but we must learn how to use it.

Corrie ten Boom, a concentration camp survivor imprisoned for helping Jews escape from the Nazis, tells a story about speaking at a church in Munich in 1947. It had been many years since a clerical error caused her to be released, sparing her from certain death, and she had devoted herself to traveling and speaking about the miracles God had performed in her life. Ten Boom had been preaching a message that night about God's forgiveness, and as the evening service ended, she noticed a balding, heavyset man walking toward her. Suddenly, she realized that this man had been one of the guards who had brutally tortured her and her sister, who had died in the camp.

It was the first time since her release that she had come face-to-face with one of her captors. Ten Boom was stunned as the man extended his hand to her and then asked if she would forgive him. All she could think about was the horror of what she had experienced. But she wrote:

> It could not have been many seconds that he stood there—hand held out—but to me it seemed hours as I wrestled with the most difficult thing I had ever had to do.
>
> For I had to do it—I knew that. The message that God forgives has a prior condition: that we forgive those who have injured us. "If you do not forgive men their trespasses," Jesus says, "neither will your father in heaven forgive your trespasses."
>
> …But forgiveness is not an emotion—I knew that too. Forgiveness is an act of the will, and the will can function regardless of the temperature of the heart. *Jesus, help me!* I prayed silently. *I can lift my hand. I can do that much. You supply the feeling.*
>
> And so woodenly, mechanically, I thrust my hand into the one stretched out to me. And as I did, an incredible thing took place. The current started in my shoulder, raced down my arm, sprang into our joined hands. And then this healing warmth seemed to flood my whole being, bringing tears to my eyes.
>
> "I forgive you, brother!" I cried. "With all my heart."[2]

If God can empower Corrie ten Boom to forgive a prison guard from a Nazi concentration camp, He can empower us to do whatever we need to do to succeed and even thrive in politics. The antidote for the hatred, selfishness, and lack of integrity we see in government and politics is for truly committed Christians living out their faith to enter the arena and apply what they have been taught and empowered by God to do in that environment. Lead by example, forgive, show love even when you are hated, fight evil, speak the truth, stand up for what is right, defend the weak and the powerless—isn't this what we are called to do as Christians? Where could this be more needed than in our government?

By the early 1970s, most evangelicals were not involved in politics. A lot of factors may have contributed to this, such as the Scopes Monkey Trial in 1925, the Johnson Amendment in 1954, the appointment of more liberal judges to the Supreme Court, removing prayer from schools in 1962, and other influences that led to a rise in church leaders telling people that they should just pull out and focus on things like helping those in need. The prevailing attitude was that Christians needed to stay in the safe zone of faith-oriented activities they could control, and that is a mindset that continues to this day. But aren't we called to be salt and light?

There are those I refer to as "called politicians," and I humbly consider myself to be one. We hear the voice of God speak to us and guide us and are filled with a desire that is not just our own. God has called us. We are not in it for ourselves. We are called forth to serve our communities and His glory. This frequently comes as a surprise to our families and us. Entering the political arena is not always an easy choice, but when you are called, you must ask yourself this: Do I trust in the Lord and leap into this sometimes unfriendly, possibly dangerous arena, or do I keep my head down and turn a deaf ear to His command?

When I first began to sense strongly that God was calling me to the political realm, I faced tremendous resistance, not from people outside the church but from within!

After being offered an incredible internship opportunity in Washington, DC, when I was a college sophomore, the people at a Bible study I attended passionately tried to talk me out of accepting it. They warned me not to become involved in politics. Listening to them for several hours one afternoon left me stressed and feeling ill!

My flight to Washington was booked for just three days later, but after our conversations, I was full of fear. Many of them cared about me a great deal, but they kept saying things like, "If you go to Washington, you will just get corrupted yourself," or "Why on earth would you, as a Christian, want to have anything to do with politics?"

But I kept praying and decided I had to choose faith over fear. I had to make a conscious choice not to let anything stand in the way of what I believed God was calling me to do.

If God is calling *you* to serve in government or politics, don't let anyone or anything stop you! If you are a pastor, I ask you, what are you doing as the leader and spiritual figurehead of your church to foster growth in the mountain of government for those in your congregation? If you are a youth pastor, are you encouraging the young people in your flock to consider serving in government if they feel led to do so?

If there are members of your church who are called to serve in that way, will you encourage them to follow that call? As the leader of the church, you set the tone. This is why it is so important that, from the pulpit, you communicate to members of the faith community that they should not be discouraging someone called by God to public service from serving Him in that way.

Perhaps it also means that you encourage more civics training and even host trainings in your church or community. According to the Brookings Institution, which cites research conducted by political scientist Robert Putnam, there are "declining levels of civic engagement across the country."[3] It is critical to train people in what good government is all about and empower them to be more engaged civically.

According to WalletHub, "Among developed nations, the U.S. is [ranked] 26 of 35 when it comes to voter turnout. That's no surprise, considering most states don't emphasize civic education in their schools. Large proportions of the public fail even simple knowledge tests such as knowing whether one's state requires identification in order to vote."[4] The Pew Research Center reported that 2016 voter turnout in the United States ranked thirtieth among thirty-five developed nations in nationwide elections.[5]

Civic engagement is truly a place where the body of Christ must reengage. It is perfectly legal for a church to do this type of training, yet very few are doing it. Many of us have no idea what God has put into us until we step out in faith and act. The talents, abilities, and courage we find when we activate our faith can be incredible. When millions of believers are not using their talents and gifts fully, our country is the poorer for it.

I read that the beautiful Nigerian word *amachi* means "who knows but what God has brought us through this child."[6] *Amachi* is about having hope. If you have a high-school or college-age student under your roof right now, they may be the very one God has called to do something great in the arena of government or politics. They may be the *amachi*.

A big reason so many churches shy away from politics is the Johnson Amendment. This amendment, named after then senator Lyndon B. Johnson, came about because, as *National Catholic Reporter* senior analyst Thomas Reese wrote, Johnson was angry "that a tax-exempt organization was supporting his opponent during an election. In response, he offered what became known as the Johnson Amendment in 1954, which prohibited nonprofit 501(c)(3) tax-exempt organizations from participating in campaigns for political office. If a tax-exempt organization violates this prohibition, it can lose its tax-exempt status, which means it would be subject to taxation and donations would not be tax deductible."[7]

The Johnson Amendment has made churches and faith-based nonprofits so afraid to speak out that it has crippled the body of Christ for decades, preventing almost any political involvement. The irony of this is that George Reedy, Johnson's chief aide in 1954, was once asked about the events surrounding the passage of the Johnson Amendment and said that Johnson "was very thin-skinned" and that it was "entirely possible" that he moved for the amendment to the tax code in response to his political adversaries. Reedy added, however, that his personal opinion was that "Johnson would never have sought restrictions on religious organizations."[8]

According to Reedy, Johnson never intended to censor churches and Christians from the political process, but that is basically what has happened. All these years later, we are still operating under a law that is frequently misinterpreted but nonetheless is effective at keeping Christians almost completely separated from the processes that determine everything important that touches their lives. Removing Christians from the process leads to politics being even dirtier, which leads to Christians wanting even less to do with it. And the vicious cycle continues.

In his famous "Farewell Address," George Washington believed so strongly that people of faith were needed in government that he said:

> Of all the dispositions and habits which lead to political prosperity, religion and morality are indispensable supports....And let us, with caution, indulge the supposition that morality can be maintained without religion....Reason and experience both forbid us to expect that national morality can prevail into the exclusion of religious principle.[9]

A lot of people enter politics for nothing but selfish reasons, no doubt. However, some enter the political arena out of obedience and a desire to serve, not selfish ambition. They often view themselves as statesmen or stateswomen. A statesman is defined as one who is a skilled, experienced, and respected political leader or figure. Statesmen and women believe that politics should be a calling, not a career.

If you feel called to politics, what should you do? Where do you start? First, you need to pray and ask others to pray for you. Having a team of committed intercessors who support you and your family during your campaign or your time in office is imperative. Be sure you are hearing God's directive correctly. I had to stop and examine my own motives thoroughly when I was making the decision to run. You also have to ask yourself this: Am I doing this because I want to *do something*, or am I just trying to *be somebody*? Am I listening to God's voice or the sound of my own ego?

If you *are* truly called to serve in politics, then you are one of the *best* equipped people to deal with what comes up in politics, and here is why: as a Christian, you have the Spirit of God. The Bible says that one of the ministries of the Holy Spirit is to teach us all things, including things related to politics and governance and leadership. So we have the Spirit of God, who is ready and willing to teach us if we humble ourselves and open up to Him.

Second, we have the wisdom that comes from the Word of God. There is no issue, situation, or question that we can't find an answer for somewhere in the Bible. Because we are God's children and have access to His wisdom and Spirit, that puts us in the position of being better equipped to handle the difficult situations of life—and yes, even the difficulties of politics. Is what we face in politics really so different from what others face when they are encountering persecution? I think not.

In addition, what also makes us unique as Christians is that we find our identity in an objective source: Jesus Christ. With our identity being in that source, we can be at peace even in the midst of turmoil, even in the midst of chaos, even in the midst of heavy decision-making.

True followers of Christ are better equipped to know how to deal with things like unforgiveness and wanting to retaliate against someone who has hurt them. The world does not have a theology of forgiveness; it has a theology of resentment. Christians are commanded to forgive and are more accountable because of the standards God holds His children to regarding love and compassion for others. If you are going into public service, love and compassion need to be a part of *why* you do what you do. While we may not always agree with others' behaviors, we are called to love and give dignity to humanity because we are the only creation made in the image of God, the *Imago Dei*.

The Bible says that one of the ministries of the Holy Spirit is to teach us all things, and that includes things related to politics, governance, and leadership. We have the Spirit of God, who is ready and willing to teach us if we humble ourselves and open up to Him. We also have the wisdom that comes from the Word of God. Answers to every question, issue, or situation in life can be found in the Bible. Because we are God's children and have access to His wisdom, we are the best equipped if we are called to be involved in politics or any other field. Christians cannot rely solely on calling, however. To enter the political arena, we must be called *and* trained *and* supported! And those who are called need to be obedient to that call.

For people who are called with the right heart and mindset, it can take years to build up the experience needed to truly be effective. Part of the right mindset is getting past the assumption that feeling called to run means you are guaranteed to win. I have a colleague who decided, against his own logic and against all odds, to run as a Republican in a historically Democrat-controlled area because he felt that God was calling him to do it. He didn't win. But what is remarkable is that he lost by a very narrow margin, just 200 votes to be exact, and he captured

49.9 percent of the ballots. This was a total shock to most people who had written off that district as one in which a conservative Republican could never be elected.

Even though my colleague's opponent attacked him constantly, he refused to stoop to her level, and the people in the district began to see her true nature emerge because of her attacks. She gerrymandered the district and did everything she could to oppose him. Because he was humble and stood his ground and told the truth, his response highlighted the tactics she was using, which turned a lot of people off to her.

Even though my friend lost, he lost by a very slim margin. And because the election was so close, it encouraged more conservative Republicans to run in the next election. In about three years, because more people were emboldened to run, all the county leaders, state senators, and House members slowly started being replaced. They are *all* Republican now.

We may not understand why God is calling us to run, but we still need to be obedient to His direction and get in the race! As Wayne Gretzky put it, "You miss 100% of the shots you don't take." In politics, it is the same. You may not win, but you will definitely lose 100 percent of the races you never enter!

Most people who run for office or enter politics believe that they must work in the preexisting system and operate under its rules alone. As Christians, however, we are called to do everything with a kingdom mindset. Entrepreneur and pastor Billy Epperhart defines this mindset: "Someone with a Kingdom mindset cares about the poor, needy, and brokenhearted. They devote their lives to the service of others.

They aren't viewed as self-righteous or hypocritical because they're too busy loving others. Someone with a Kingdom mindset will also recklessly abandon anything for the sake of the gospel. They realize that following the voice of the Holy Spirit is **the** most important thing (Matthew 13:44)."[10]

If God calls you or me to run for a political office, we need to be so assured by His guidance that when the opposition attacks, we respond with a different mindset— a kingdom mindset. This requires a great deal of training, both spiritually and professionally, to develop wisdom, maturity, and the skill set to know how to handle what will be thrown at you.

Most candidates do not have the time to micromanage their campaigns and decide who prints the yard signs and provides coffee and donuts at the campaign headquarters. This means that the first thing a candidate must do after throwing their hat in the ring is choose people to lead the campaign, raise money, and run the on-the-ground daily activities. Decision-making and even financial decisions, by necessity, must be assigned to someone else most of the time.

Who do they turn to for counsel? Most candidates hire consultants who are recommended to them. In my experience, those referrals were not the most effective. Even though some of my consultants were very good and did a terrific job, others took advantage of me terribly. One of the most important decisions you can make as a candidate is whom you will hire to run your campaign, because political consultants can quite often be kingmakers and can make or break a candidate.

If they are highly experienced, they can steer resources, influence, valuable relationships, and potential donors and

PAC money to whichever candidate they choose to promote. So if they care about nothing other than taking on the candidates who will make them the most money, this is a major threat to our ability to have good government.

As American citizens, we are enabling a system that contributes heavily toward promoting our leaders, with money often being the only driver. If our leaders are hand selected by people who often do not have the best interests of the country, the state, or the legislative district at heart, the people will continue to suffer.

Political consultants are certainly not the only influence on who gets elected, but they definitely play a role. Perhaps we need more godly people who will come alongside those running for office to serve as political consultants and advisors. We need those who desire to see good leaders put in place more than anything else and who will value something other than just money. We as the body of Christ need to raise up a new standard not just regarding the quality of the candidates we are supporting but also in regard to the consultants and others who stand behind those candidates.

Perhaps the world of politics needs more "armor bearers" and honest brokers who will participate in this activity and treat it with the seriousness and reverence that this country deserves. If God calls you to be a political consultant or someone who works in the sphere of politics, you may literally be helping shape the future of our nation. Choose wisely who you invest in as leaders, and make it about something bigger than just yourself.

Your team can truly make or break you, so candidates *must* do their homework before announcing their decision to run. Talk to people who have gotten elected and ask them about their experience with consultants, media advisers, strategists, and vendors. Lining up these people ahead of time is very important. Ask like-minded Christians for recommendations on who to trust and who to avoid.

Also consider asking for references from any consultant you are thinking of hiring. Don't just talk to their former clients who have won. Ask to talk to the candidates who hired them and lost. Would they hire this consultant again? If so, why? If someone who lost would hire that person again, that is a very good sign that they did their job correctly. Consultants and vendors have to be paid just like everyone else, but this is another case where a major donor could make a huge difference by putting up the much-needed funds for a candidate to hire top-notch people who have already been vetted. That will truly give a solid candidate the advantage they need.

CHAPTER 11

TRAINED

*If you know the enemy and know yourself, you need
not fear the result of a hundred battles. If you know
yourself but not the enemy, for every victory gained
you will also suffer a defeat. If you know neither the
enemy nor yourself, you will succumb in every battle.*

—Sun Tzu

RON PIERCE IS a former captain with the Sacramento Metropolitan Fire District. As a veteran firefighter for more than forty-one years, Pierce has trained thousands of other firefighters.

> As a captain of a crew going into a burning structure with thick black smoke, I know the fear of the unknown inside and all the things that can go bad instantly. My fear is not only for myself but for my crew as I am making decisions where I have my own life and the lives of my crew in my hands. Our "fight or flight" mechanism in our brains is always functioning as we observe everything around us; our vision is very limited, and the sounds are very intimidating. Scared? Yes. Frightened? Yes. Job to do? Yes! SAFE? That's the million-dollar question, but a decision must be made—go in or retreat. Our training keeps us safe and helps us know the right answer.[1]

Pierce shared with me that the training for a recruit, or a "rookie," starts with teaching them to overcome their natural instinct, which is to run away from the intense heat and blinding smoke that one encounters when running into a burning building. He explained that "their skill at overcoming their fears is due to training. We put a new firefighter from off the street, that comes into the academy, through a long training process. And then, once they come out of the academy, they're put on probation for almost a year. Everybody knows that person is new and that they may not want to go in that door when they enter a fire for the first time. But once they've been through training, learned to rely on their safety gear, and over time, experienced a hot environment, they begin to realize how effective, even with fire coming at them, their protective clothing, breathing apparatus, hose line, and other equipment are, and they gain confidence. They are put through training to learn to override their natural instincts."[2]

Rookies begin by entering a room registering a temperature of about 850 degrees when they first go through the door. They never go in alone. The captain and other trained firefighters are with them at all times. They are outfitted with their two most valuable pieces of equipment, their turnouts and breathing apparatus. A firefighter's suit is called his "turnout gear" and is designed to withstand flames and extremely high temperatures (fires can burn at up to 2000 degrees) but only for short periods of time.[3]

Pierce explained, "The breathing apparatus, that's very foreign to them when they are new. You have a tank on your back and a breathing mask and a face shield over your mask. It can be claustrophobic. And there's smoke, a lot of smoke, but they begin to feel confident over time, realizing that the smoke will not hurt them because they have their breathing apparatus and face shield, which protects their eyes. Then as time goes on, we increase the smoke. We make it black. The next step is to introduce some heat. We then introduce some actual flames. As they inch closer to the source of the fire, the heat increases more and more. The room they are placed in can be as much as 5,000 degrees at the very back, but part of what comes with their training is learning what they can and cannot handle.

"We will test that recruit in a lot of ways because there are so many different scenarios you can have with fire. Every day is different, and every fire always has some curve that it throws at you."

Pierce went on to say, "It's a constant thing with us, even those of us that have been in service for a long time. We have to recognize the dangers and not get overconfident. You really never stop training. It's just constant training, and you learn every day." He said this after he'd been a firefighter for forty-one years.

Also, Pierce shared the number one mistake most untrained people make when they find themselves in a fire—they stand up and try to run. "That is the worst thing you can do," he said. "Smoke rises, so if you stand up, you're going to inhale more smoke, and that can cost you your life." So he said, "What you have to do is stay low and find safety zones where if things go bad, you can retreat to those areas where the fire won't be as dangerous." He further explained, "Fear is the biggest killer in a fire because you panic. You might stand up, and you might lose all sense of where the doors are."

As a Christian who has been in the political arena most of my life, the parallels of what Pierce described here are truly remarkable. No one would dispute that firefighting is a dangerous business. Politics is very much the same. But with proper training for either profession, you can enter even the most difficult and sometimes dangerous circumstances and come out unscathed.

This is what I believe God is calling more Christians to do. If you are truly willing to be obedient to His voice, then get trained. Learn how much heat is too much. Establish safety zones for yourself and retreat to them often if necessary. And by all means, first and foremost, stay low. Stay humble. This should not be about you. It's about being called. It's about service. It's about being obedient. If it ever becomes about you, it's time to get out. There is no place in God's kingdom for pride. You also need to remember not to step into the arena as a politician without your spiritual armor!

If you truly believe God is calling you to run for office or serve in government, in most circumstances you also must be trained. Many well-meaning Christians have been unsuccessful because even though they may have felt called, they were not trained. The two must go hand in hand.

William Borden, heir to the Borden Dairy fortune, graduated from high school in 1904. For his graduation present, his parents gave him a trip around the world. As he traveled throughout Asia, the Middle East, and Europe, he felt a growing desire to become a missionary. When he returned from that trip, legend goes, he wrote two words on the back of his Bible: "No reserves." He decided he was not going to hold anything back from the Lord.

He felt called, and what did he do next? He went to school. In 1905, he left for Yale, where he spent four years preparing himself. While in college, he wrote something in his journal that embodied his life: "Say 'no' to self and 'yes' to Jesus every time."

After he graduated, again according to legend, he wrote two more words on the back of his Bible: "No retreats." He then studied at Princeton Seminary in New Jersey, and when he completed his work there, he finally made plans to go to China.

He was ready and prepared to go into the mission field, said goodbye to his family, and left for

> *Many well-meaning Christians have been unsuccessful because even though they may have felt called, they were not trained. The two must go hand in hand.*

China. On his way there, he stopped in Egypt, where sadly, he contracted spinal meningitis and died. After his death, his family reportedly found his Bible and saw that he had written two more words on the back: "No regrets." He was a man who lived by those three declarations: no reserves, no retreats, and no regrets.[4]

Was Borden's life a failure because he never made it to China to serve as a missionary? No, because in the end, his courage and the way he lived inspired thousands of people to go into the mission field! In her book *Borden of Yale '09*, Mrs. Howard Taylor asserts that he was celebrated as someone who "not only gave (away) his wealth but himself, in a way so joyous and natural that it (seemed) a privilege rather than a sacrifice." The key thing is, he had the call of God on his life, and he was determined to be obedient to that call. Once he knew he was called, he prepared himself for that calling.

When Sang Yi, a Fairfax City, Virginia, councilman, wanted to get involved in politics, he approached a friend who was an elected official and told him he wanted to run for office. His friend told him, "OK, but I want you to do three things for me first." He said, "Number one, I want you to go join your homeowners' association, and I want you to become its president. The second thing I want you to do is I want you to join the American Legion or the Veterans of Foreign Wars or some military organization." Then he said, "After you do these two things, I'm going to help you get on a board or commission in your government."

Yi did all three things. He said the first one was the most horrible thing he had ever done. "If you can make it through being your HOA president, you can make it being in office! It is an excellent litmus test that turned out to be a great experience because if you get 51 percent of your neighborhood to still like you after that then you probably have a good chance of being elected!"

He also found that he made friends with many fellow veterans in the American Legion, and he became a second vice commander. He said, "I loved every minute of it and met some wonderful people." He realized that becoming involved with these groups wasn't just about preparing to run for office anymore, it was about being part of his community. Being active and being present was an incredibly fulfilling experience.

Yi was then appointed to serve on the Virginia Alcohol Safety Action policy board, which helped him better understand how government works. He realized that a lot of good things were happening in his community after all, and it affirmed his desire to be a public servant because he came to love the people and the places he was serving. Isn't that what public service is supposed to be about?

If you are called to serve in government, learn more about participating in public service and identify the places where you can be trained. In the back of this book, you will find a list of some amazing organizations working to train Christians to enter the world of politics. Just as with anything else in life, you must seek to understand a problem to be effective at solving it.

Organizations like the Leadership Institute, Kingdom in Politics, the Family Policy Alliance, the Wilberforce Alliance, the LBJ Women's Campaign School, the D. James Kennedy Center for Christian Leadership, and others provide excellent training opportunities. You should also plug into trainings from the Republican National Committee or the Democratic National Committee, depending on which party you affiliate with, so you can take advantage of their trainings too.

The Democratic Party used to have more conservative-leaning members called "Blue Dog Democrats." They are almost all gone now because they have been squeezed out and "canceled" by the more hardline extreme Left leaders who have taken control of the party and are pushing almost unanimously for socialism.

We need people of integrity and faith from both parties to be involved in politics. A lot of Christians have said to me, "I could never be a Democrat because there's no way that as a Christian I could support the platforms of the Democratic Party." While I completely understand this logic, with fewer Christians involved in either party,

Democratic or Republican, our country will be pushed further and further away from Christian values because there will be no one there to push back.

Faith is a verb. The more good people who add their names to the ballot, the greater the likelihood one of them will win. The same is true in reverse. We must understand that this is a numbers game, and right now we are often not even playing!

If you feel God is calling you to be engaged in government and politics, what should you do? Get trained. Can you imagine if someone woke up one morning and decided they just wanted to climb Mount Everest with no previous training or experience? How well would that go? What did David do when Samuel anointed him the next king of Israel? Did he start trying to lead immediately or form a shadow government? No, he continued to be a shepherd. He continued to build his skills and his confidence in God. When the timing was right, God called him forth. Just as with any profession, you must be trained, and you must trust in God's timing, not your own.

As one political consultant friend shared with me, many of her clients often feel passionate about wanting to serve and may even feel called, but they think they can simply jump into this profession with little or no training and be successful. It simply doesn't work that way! Even if you have the financial resources to self-fund your campaign, running for office yourself may not be the best use of those resources. Pray and ask God to show you if that money may be better spent helping others who are called and highly trained in the political arena but may lack the financial resources to succeed.

If you are not trained, you could do more harm than good by entering into political roles or debates without understanding everything about the environment or arena into which you are stepping. Just because you feel strongly about an issue does not mean you understand all the complexities involved to move policy forward. Just because you feel called to run for office doesn't mean you will always win, and it may not mean that you are supposed to run right now. Politics must be approached with strategy, precision, and spiritual discernment because your opposition may gain the upper hand if you are not adequately prepared.

If you feel God has called you to be a lawyer, what do you have ahead of you? Well, you've got to finish your undergraduate program, go through three years of law school, and perhaps be a paralegal or clerk for someone. If you feel like God's called you to be a surgeon, what do you have ahead of you? Nine years of medical school and a residency program. If you feel God's calling you to any other profession, they all involve some kind of training, so the answer to God's call is, "All right, Lord, if You're calling me to do this, I want to get equipped. I want to study to show myself approved. Please show me how I need to do that."

We in the body need to encourage people to follow where God is leading them as they use their gifts, callings, and stirrings in their hearts to serve in this way. Why wouldn't the body of Christ be an advocate for the engagement of God's people to pursue these types of endeavors? Isn't that the *only* way we will begin to have more voices in high places? More voices in the arenas of decision-making?

> The LORD God is my strength, and he will make my
> feet like hinds' feet, and he will make me to walk
> upon mine high places.
>
> —HABAKKUK 3:19, KJV

The mountain of government is not for the faint of heart, and it takes a great deal of discipline and training to develop hinds' feet. As author Sara Cain puts it, "A hind is a female deer that can place her back feet exactly where her front feet stepped. Not one inch off! In times of danger, she is able to run securely and not get 'off track.' She is able to scale unusually high and difficult terrain to elude predators. She is able to run with abandonment and not fear."[5]

Perhaps you are not called to run for office, but you want to get involved and become more active in the public square to make a difference in your community, city, or state. Start with learning public speaking because it is a critical skill to be effective in any meeting or event. You need to know how you want to frame your message if you are a concerned parent, for example, who is speaking out in a county meeting about an education issue or a policy change.

Passion has a role, but facts and stories are even more powerful. So when you have your three to five minutes at the microphone, you need to structure your comments so that you will be effective.

As with anything else, practice and skill are how you make an impact. Do your homework, get trained, learn to get comfortable with public speaking, and then get involved! Ask the hard, awkward questions of your leaders. There is strength in numbers, so get others to ask too.

For example, let's say that you would like to communicate

with your congressional representative about an issue. Often, Congress members and their staff are overwhelmed with daily responsibilities, but there are ways that we, as average citizens, can best communicate with them and even help prepare them for making good policy decisions.

You need to know your audience. The Congressional Management Foundation (CMF) has very helpful resources, and I have included a list of some of them in the appendix of this book. If you are communicating with a member of Congress, certain things are way more effective than others. Form letters, online mass petitions, and other types of communication that are impersonal typically are less effective.

Personalized emails that come from you as a constituent are much more effective than form emails. However, the two most effective ways to communicate with a Congress member or their staff are, hands down, a personal handwritten letter or, even better, an in-person meeting.

According to a survey conducted by CMF, "Most of the congressional staff surveyed said constituent visits to the Washington office (97%) and to the district/state office (94%) have 'some' or 'a lot' of influence on an undecided Member, more than any other influence group or strategy."[6] From my experience, I have learned that if you want to be successful with people in the media, for example, you do everything you can to help them save time when writing a story. You give them well-researched facts and information ahead of their deadlines, and you build a relationship with them so there is a higher level of trust.

It is no different when dealing with members of Congress, state legislators, city council members, or your local mayor. They are always pressed for time, and if you have their attention, the better prepared you are the more effective you will be at getting them to really listen. Reading through hundreds of pages of information is something most elected officials rarely have the time to do, so come prepared to leave behind a clear and concise one- to two-page summary that will help them know your concerns.

As a constituent, don't be afraid to keep in touch with your congressional representative. It's a good idea to touch base every once in a while, but don't be what congressional staff call a "pen pal" or someone who overcommunicates with them.[7] You should contact your representative's office to call their attention to an issue that concerns you. If there is movement on key legislation in committee, or if a major vote is expected, you can remind the legislator of your stance. CMF affirms that "if communications are informative, respectful, concise and direct, they can go a long way toward helping the Member and staffer keep the issue on their radar."[8]

Finally, I will close with this from another recent CMF report: "From the founding of our country, in-person meetings with Senators and Representatives have been the most effective way for citizens to shape public policy. Even with the many and diverse communications venues now available, meetings still trump any other interaction between legislators and their constituents. Anyone who wishes to help shape public policy on the issues about which they care deeply should consider scheduling meetings with their Senators and Representatives."[9] Average people can make a difference just by getting involved. It may be as simple as calling a congressman's or senator's office and requesting a meeting!

CHAPTER 12

SUPPORTED

Seek first to understand, then to be understood.
—STEPHEN R. COVEY

A s AMERICANS, WE tend to attack the fruit and not the roots of what is happening in our country. The television is full of people speaking out with incredible frustration about the fruit of bad policy decisions and corrupt leaders. Often, it seems that dismal results and failures abound. But no one is talking about what is *really* causing these things.

Working for a freshman member of Congress when I was in my twenties was one of my most rewarding and eye-opening experiences. It was also one of the most grueling. Often, I worked seventy to eighty hours a week when Congress was in session, sometimes more. It was not uncommon to arrive back at my office at seven o'clock some mornings after having gone home at two a.m. I would drive home, get three or four hours of sleep, take a shower, put on fresh clothes, and hurry to be back before the boss arrived. If he was going down to the floor of the US House of Representatives that morning with my talking points or to vote on something in my issue area, I knew I had to be there the minute he walked in that door. I had to brief him and ensure he had what he needed.

As a brand-new legislative assistant, I was making

$28,000 a year while living in one of the most expensive cities in the world. I barely made enough to pay my rent and buy a few groceries. At that time, most Hill staffers like me typically lived off of the food served at the receptions held almost every evening somewhere on the Capitol complex. Necessity made us organized, and we would call each other around four thirty or five p.m. to share which receptions were going to have the best food. Years later, my friends and I still joke that had it not been for those receptions, we might have starved!

That was back in the late nineties, and one of the most astonishing things I have uncovered in my research for this book is that the salaries for Hill staffers doing the exact same job I did are not much higher now than they were then!

What *has* changed, however, is the workload. According to the Pew Research Center, the House of Representatives has one voting member for every 747,000 or so Americans. And because of the latest census numbers, the Census Bureau reports that this number is about to jump to 761,000 people! "That's by far the highest population-to-representative ratio among a peer group of industrialized democracies, and the highest it's been in U.S. history," Pew reported.[1] The average number of people a member serves has continued to rise steadily. In fact, as of 2018, the United States had the highest citizen-to-representative ratio of all Organization for Economic Co-operation and Development (OECD) nations around the world. The US population keeps growing, but the US House of Representatives is the same size as it was during the Taft era.[2]

The editors of the book *Congress Overwhelmed* make

a disturbing statement: "The claim is that Congress lacks the basic knowledge resources to perform its legislative and oversight duties well. Individual members and their staff simply don't have the time and expertise to adequately understand the public problems they are attempting to resolve. As a result, Congress is left to rely on external sources of expertise, especially from executive branch staff, whom they are supposed to check and balance, and outside lobbyists, who represent narrow, predominantly business, interests."[3]

Working on Capitol Hill is a lot like being on a big college campus that also has elements of the TV shows *Survivor, The Apprentice,* and *Shark Tank,* with a little bit of strategy by Sun Tzu thrown in for good measure. Add all that together and it can make for quite a pressure cooker, which is why the average turnover of Congressional staffers is roughly three years.[4] Most people simply burn out after a very short time because of the sheer exhaustion that stems from such an intense work environment.

However, knowing how Congress works and understanding how our nation's policies are formed is something that every young person interested in our government should seek to experience. I encourage everyone who is high school or college age to consider doing an internship on Capitol Hill or in the White House or a federal agency. In the back of this book, I have included a list of organizations that help place young people in good internships. Washington is truly a remarkable place where you will see the best and the worst in people, but the skills and knowledge you gain there will serve you the rest of your life.

All the pressure that members of Congress as well as

their staffs are under from just the work stress alone, in addition to the fact that Capitol Hill breeds a lot of internecine battles, makes it an incredibly difficult place to work. But it is also one of the most incredible places on the planet to make a difference. The connections you make, the skills you learn, and the knowledge you gain about how our government operates are invaluable. It also gives one a better understanding of how decisions are made and what really drives public policy. If you are called to politics, this type of firsthand training is critical. Even if you are not called to serve in this way, it is always helpful to know how your government works.

To deal with the root causes of some of the issues we are facing, we must first seek to truly understand the problems and then stop supporting those things that are fueling them. What would our government look like if we only supported people who are truly called to politics and are properly trained?

We, as average citizens, need to invest more in our government on a daily basis because if we don't, others who may not share our values will. Christians pray that God will raise up people who will lead us with biblical values, but what are we doing to support them and their staffs when they are campaigning or after they get into office?

Our investment can take many forms. First and foremost, start with prayer and direct involvement as we have discussed in previous chapters. Investment also means making certain that you are participating and paying attention to what is being discussed and debated.

The only way to root out the corruption and rampant self-benefiting behavior of so many of our political leaders is for more people to enter the arena who have a common goal of wanting to foster good government and good policy decisions. After all, as we discussed before, this is a numbers game and most honest people who are there simply to serve are quite often outnumbered. This may seem overwhelming to those who have tried to go it alone, but it is not so overwhelming if we approach it as a body—*the* body.

My first job on Capitol Hill was helping former House speaker Newt Gingrich drain the congressional swamp. As part of the senior leadership team for the newly created chief administrative officer (CAO) for the House of Representatives, we immediately went to work to bring reforms to the broken and often unaccounted for financial systems and taxpayer-funded operations of Congress.

For example, when decades of old furniture belonging to the House of Representatives, and thus the American people, was discovered sitting in a dusty warehouse in Washington with no purpose, we did something truly outside the box: we held a yard sale on the front steps of a federal government building and auctioned everything off! After cleaning out the warehouse and closing it down, the savings to the taxpayers totaled $235,000 per year from just that basic step of getting rid of old, useless furniture. That was just the beginning.

Our team then pushed for the first independent audit of the House since 1789, the year George Washington was first inaugurated as president. This audit shined the brightest of spotlights on Congress, unleashing historic changes and reforms and using business-minded approaches when spending taxpayers' money. These unprecedented reforms called out politics as usual and resulted in the core operations of the people's House having much greater accountability and transparency. According to the former CAO, Scot Faulkner, because of these reforms, American taxpayers saved approximately $184 million per year, [5] or more than $4.4 billion to date! The measures were recognized as one of the top one hundred reforms in American government and have since served as a model for other governments around the world.[6] Holding government accountable and fighting for conservative values is desperately needed; but often, average people don't understand the critical role they play in helping to make that happen.

Sometimes the best way to support a public figure is to hold them accountable. So often, those in elected leadership positions find it more and more challenging to take a hard stand. As you become more senior and are appointed or elected to higher-level roles, the battles become more difficult, and often, complex things are happening below the surface around a decision. It baffles the public that certain decisions are made because they only have limited amounts of information. As my former boss Scot Faulkner used to jokingly say, "In politics, you should never let rational thinking get in the way of a good decision."

For example, if a leader has a vocal constituent base that is calling for action on certain issues, their outcry can make it much easier for that person to push for those things behind the scenes. It provides the leader cover. If the constituent base is not doing its job by watching what is happening, speaking out about issues and concerns, and calling for more action or transparency, then it is much more difficult for the leader to fight without that support.

If more average people pushed for independent audits,

for instance, this would be an effective way to create a lot more transparency in government. If the public outcry is very high and does not let up, it is extremely difficult for public figures to ignore that forever. We are not properly exercising our right to hold our leaders accountable, which in some ways is the very best way to support them.

Paying your dues and being part of a membership organization like Concerned Women for America, the National Right to Life Committee, or the 60 Plus Association is good, but at the end of the day, there is just no substitute for personal involvement in your government at every level in some form or fashion. It is one thing to get the right people elected to office; it is quite another for them to be supported once they get in. Once you peek behind the curtain, often those who are serving as representatives or senators, on the state or federal level, do not have enough staff support to keep up with everything they need to know to make informed decisions. They are lacking the grassroots support needed to counteract the enormous pressure they will be under from special interest groups. So if we want to impact policy decisions, we can no longer sit back and assume that others are going to correctly tell them about the issues we care about.

Many of us need to develop a less adversarial relationship with our leaders and find ways to support them. Perhaps it's time to quit complaining and just get to work! This may mean forming groups that research specific topics using thoroughly vetted, credible sources, then summarizing those findings and presenting them to your government leaders. Consider making a presentation in a meeting with their office to let them know there is strong constituent support on that issue. It may also mean speaking out publicly at town hall meetings, radio interviews, etc. This is the only way to counterbalance some of the impact of paid lobbyists who currently provide research or policy suggestions for those in government with their own interests in mind. Often, the only people who are providing information for those in decision-making positions in government are paid to do so and have very specific agendas that are almost always geared toward benefiting a company or a special interest. By getting more directly involved, average citizens can push back against this type of one-sided process and allow lawmakers to hear from all sides.

> *We are not properly exercising our right to hold our leaders accountable, which in some ways is the very best way to support them.*

Another common misperception by people who are not involved in politics directly is the belief that elected officials live the high life. They think they spend most of their time attending fancy parties, taking expensive trips, and being wined and dined. Yes, some of that is true. But what is also true is that a lot of what happens in politics is incredibly draining, tremendously stressful, and quite often puts you in situations that are difficult for an honest person because it is very hard to stand up against corruption and compromise. This is also why you must be called to do this because if God has not called and equipped you, you will not be able to stand up under that kind of pressure.

Many people understand the importance of helping get

someone good elected. They may even work hard, give money, and vote. But why is it that once their candidate wins and is placed in a position of authority, most people assume they are no longer needed and move on? Believe it or not, they need you just as much *after* they get elected as before.

Let's say, for instance, that you have done your homework, said your prayers, given your time, money, and influence, and your candidate wins a seat for federal office. Now they are being sent to Washington! Most people think they have now done all they need to do and stop showing any care or concern for that person. But the truth is that after that person wins, they need you and your prayers and support more than ever.

Put yourself in their shoes for a moment. They're suddenly in a strange city, having to spend a great deal of their time in Washington. On a daily, even hourly, basis, people are attempting to influence them, sometimes in the wrong ways. Often, they are separated from all or part of their family for days on end, and they work long, grueling hours that, over time, can take quite a toll on a family.

Not everything about being an elected official is glamorous. Having worked on Capitol Hill for six years, I can tell you that much of it is not. It requires constant vigilance (and support) to stay the course. Most freshmen members of Congress don't even have a place to live when they first arrive. They often stay in a hotel for weeks and weeks on end. Recently, a freshman member's wife said to me, "Gosh, it was so nice. Last week, we had a Christian ministry leader invite us over to his house for a dinner that his wife was kind enough to prepare for us. It was the first home-cooked meal we had eaten in weeks." Another freshman member's spouse shared with me that when they moved to Washington, all the ladies in her Bible study back home each wrote her a personal note. Then they mailed them all to her at once. She said she read every word of each of them, and it meant so much to her that they took the time to do that. Members of Congress and their spouses are still people, and they need our support.

Recently, another congressional wife was very candid with me in a conversation we had over lunch. She said, "My husband has one of the only jobs in the world where people are paid to try and get him to sleep with them! Lobbyists are paid to come in his office constantly trying to get him to support a bill, and they will do anything to get him to do that. They will send attractive women in just to try and get him to have affairs with them so he will then do what they want."

How do you expect a marriage to survive in that kind of environment unless you have been trained to have some idea of what you are about to face, have a lot of discipline in the marriage, and have very strict integrity? I'm happy to report that my friend and her husband have stayed happily married for many years because they anticipated many of the issues and pitfalls that might come up and have put safeguards in place to protect their marriage. Elected officials contend with many things that average people do not. That is all the more reason why they need training *and* support. It is time for the body of Christ to lean in on a whole new level.

At some point, we Christians are the ones who are accountable for what is happening because we're not shoring these leaders up. We're not doing what we need to do to support them the minute they get into office. So often, when someone gets elected, people ignore them until they do something wrong, and then all they hear is criticism. When did you last look for something one of your elected officials did right and publicly praise them for it?

Remember them, their spouse, and their kids in your prayers because after election night, many times their challenges are just beginning. And remember that we are called to do way more than just pray.

> "My God sent his angel, and he shut the mouths of the lions. They have not hurt me, because I was found innocent in his sight. Nor have I ever done any wrong before you, Your Majesty." The king was overjoyed and gave orders to lift Daniel out of the den. And when Daniel was lifted from the den, no wound was found on him, because he had trusted in his God.
>
> —DANIEL 6:22–23

Another little-known fact is that within the sphere of government and politics, there is often an overwhelming element of isolation. Unfortunately, politics attracts many people who want to get close to leaders to broker the information and access they will gain from them. And quite frequently, we hold our leaders to an impossible standard. A common fear is that if you step out of isolation and trust others with what you are really feeling or struggling with, it will bring betrayal. If you are called to be in politics, isolation can be one of the toughest pieces to navigate because as humans we're created for community and to be in relationships with others. We are commanded to "bear one another's burden," but many times, those who have the most tremendous burdens—often making decisions that impact thousands of lives—cannot talk about or let others into the struggles they face while making those decisions.

Frequently, politics creates an atmosphere where many believe it is best to trust no one and become almost totally self-reliant. After all, "Knowledge is power."[7] The higher up you go, the more isolated and difficult it becomes. Many times, you are placed in situations where it's hard to get your needs met in the right ways, which makes it easier to slip into getting them met the wrong way. The saying "If you want a friend in Washington, get a dog" starts to feel like truth after you quickly realize everyone wants to be your friend when you are in a position of authority, but rarely can most of those "friends" be trusted.

While it is true that you would be foolish to trust most people who surround you in politics, political leaders are still human and face the same struggles others do every day. Keep this proverb in mind: "If you want to go fast, go alone. If you want to go far, go together."

What can we, as the body, do to go together with our leaders to best support those people who are in office? One interesting model for this may be found with a nonprofit based in North Carolina called Warrior Family Ministries (WFM). WFM provides chaplain services to veterans, law enforcement personnel, first responders, and military members. Chaplains are subject to a lot of stress themselves because they often minister to people who are dealing with severe post-traumatic stress disorder (PTSD), suffering from severe trauma, and in some cases experiencing suicidal thoughts and making attempts on their own life.

Here is what makes WFM unique: cofounder Brenda Swartz believes that it is just as important to support and minister to the men and women who are in leadership roles in her organization, the chaplains, as it is to reach out to the people they are ministering to each day. Chaplains are trained to support other chaplains in specific ways that allow them to deal with the enormous pressures of their jobs. Everything they share with each other is kept in the strictest confidence. When you are in a role where you are expected to be giving and giving, you must have others there to help refill you or you will burn out. WFM also provides a large team of intercessors who pray for each chaplain on a regular basis and are "on call" if special prayer needs arise. Because they recognize that the pressures of their jobs are enormous, they have built-in "safety nets" to help chaplains deal with that pressure in the best ways possible. The program has built in a variety of emotional safety nets, spiritual safety nets, and physical safety nets.

This is an amazing model because it speaks to the undergirding that people in leadership positions require in a way that anticipates their needs before they even arise. Can you imagine what it might do for our political leaders if we did the same thing for them as the body of Christ? Imagine if every member of Congress (and each of their spouses) had their own highly trained DC-based chaplain. Right now, there is one chaplain for the House and one for the Senate. That means two people serve 535 people. If you include congressional spouses in that number, those two chaplains serve close to 1,000 people. While many of those serving in

Congress have their own pastors or trusted spiritual advisers back in their home districts, many come to Washington and do not have that type of local support system.

As the body, we have often failed to support our leaders, and we are seeing the fruit of this. Instead of complaining about the fruit, we need to go to the roots. We need to ask the Lord, "What is my assignment and alignment with my government leaders?" In every situation, in every relationship, in every decision our leaders make, they need prayer cover and support. Just as Ron Pierce said about the firefighters he has trained, they need to learn to establish "safety zones" and retreat to them often. The good news: some small but impactful ministries serving those on Capitol Hill are trying to create those types of zones. But they can't do it alone.

Many people believe that Washington is devoid of any real Christians and that almost everyone in office is like the fictional President Frank Underwood from the Netflix series *House of Cards*. What you probably are not hearing is that there are thriving Christian ministries on Capitol Hill. Just like the faith-based organizations doing amazing work in the Mathare Valley, some are hard at work in Washington as well.

Ministries like Alabaster House and Hope to the Hill are there to support members of Congress and their staffs. Others like Well Versed, Capitol Worship, Faith and Law, the D. James Kennedy Center for Christian Statesmanship, and Cru (formerly Campus Crusade for Christ) minister not only to members of Congress but to the US Capitol Police too. I fondly remember the support and encouragement I received through one of the Center for Christian

Statesmanship Bible studies that I attended every week while working on Capitol Hill.

These ministries and others view Washington as one of the most valuable and fertile mission fields on the planet. But they could do so much more with additional support from the body through individuals and churches across the country. Consider giving to them financially and supporting them with your prayers. Pray about becoming a part of what they are doing. It should also encourage you, fellow believers, to know that there *are* Christians in Washington. God is at work, even in the halls of government. The enemy wants us to believe that there is no hope and no point in trying and that we should just leave that area to him. I am here to tell you that is a lie! There are amazing spiritual breakthroughs and battles fought with victory that happen every day in the political realm. But just as with any other kind of battle, reinforcements are needed!

I challenge you to pray about learning, navigating, and understanding relationships within the government and within the political process. Let God lead you in how best to help the people who are directly stepping into that. Believe me, if they are called and doing it for selfless reasons, they need you. Faith-filled candidates and elected officials need faith-filled people who are simply trying to serve God to come alongside them for the purpose of support, encouragement, and accountability. An ongoing partnership with people of faith can provide a source of strength for a candidate or public official that goes beyond even their own personal reservoir.

Here are some practical tips for supporting those you

believe in, have prayed about, and want to support and get behind:

1. Consider recruiting ten to twenty people of influence and financial resources to work together in your county, congressional district, or state; then look for the candidates who are the right leaders to fill critical spots to be supported by that group of people. This will give the candidate the proper resources to be fully supported and succeed.

2. Stay in touch with your candidate's campaign staff and then office staff once they are elected. Get to know them, and check in with them from time to time. Let them know that you are a constituent. Ask them how you can best be supportive.

3. Praise them publicly when they do something right. Write a letter to the editor of your local paper and the largest publication in the state.

4. Ask how you can best pray for them.

5. Ask if there are any events coming up or programs that you can be involved with or help them promote.

6. Call into radio shows that are discussing topics in line with what your candidate supports. This is your opportunity to bring up your candidate's name and talk about why

he or she is the best person for the office
they are seeking. Other listeners can become
familiar with your candidate's stand on the
issues by hearing your input.

You can say things like, "I'm so glad you're talking about this issue today. I'm calling because I just want to let you know I'm supporting _____ for Congress because he/she is strong on this issue. I have met with them, and I know it's important to him/her. I believe in him/her, and I'm asking others who really care about this issue to get behind this candidate. I'm supporting him/her because I know they are personally committed to making a difference on this issue."

Call in to shows that are interviewing your candidate so that you can throw your support behind their position. Let the listeners know the candidate has backing from voters like you, not just airtime on a radio or TV program. Your voice can help win hearts and votes, especially if you have name recognition in the community.

Attend events hosted by your elected officials in the district. Sign up for their news alerts or emails, or call their office and tell them you would like to be kept informed. A recent CMF report says, "If meeting attendees are seen visibly engaged in advocacy, and public policy in the district or state—especially in a constructive, non-confrontational way—legislators and their staff view those individuals as more trustworthy advocates for their issues. If attendees are able to plan an event or site visit for the Member, even better. The Member can see, first-hand, what the group is advocating for and, if other constituents are involved, both the issue and the Member receive broader attention."[8] The same is true for state or local officials.

Candidates, as we know, are judged by the number and high regard of their supporters. High endorsement numbers create momentum for them.

Another thing to keep in mind is *how* you support a candidate. Does your public support reflect your candidate's Christian values? Are you speaking about the positives your candidate brings to the table or bashing their opponents in ways that are not productive? As followers of Jesus, we need to reflect Him well. You could do more harm than good to a candidate by being adversarial on social media. It is all too easy to get dragged down by negative people. Resist the temptation to respond to baiting.

Psalm 15 encourages us to always take the high road.

> LORD, who may dwell in your sacred tent? Who may live on your holy mountain? The one whose walk is blameless, who does what is righteous, who speaks the truth from their heart; whose tongue utters no slander, who does no wrong to a neighbor, and casts no slur on others; who despises a vile person but honors those who fear the LORD; who keeps an oath even when it hurts, and does not change their mind; who lends money to the poor without interest; who does not accept a bribe against the innocent. Whoever does these things will never be shaken.

CHAPTER 13

THE ENEMY ON OUR DOORSTEP

Government apart from God becomes God.
—PASTOR MATTHEW MAHER

A S AN ALABAMA high school student, I was chosen to travel to the Soviet Union for the People to People international student exchange program as part of the first delegation from my home state. It shocked me to see the oppression and hopelessness of the people and their lack of choices and freedoms that most Americans take completely for granted. That experience, at such a young age, shaped my worldview and deepened my love and appreciation for the United States. After three long weeks in a Communist country, when our plane touched down at John F. Kennedy Airport, the first thing a few of my travel companions and I did was get down on our hands and knees and kiss the ground! I had never been so grateful to be an American.

In his historic book *The 5000 Year Leap*, W. Cleon Skousen talks about how the United States, in less than two hundred years, changed the course of history for the entire world by bringing modernization and establishing a civil society in a way that no other country or civilization had ever done before! Skousen writes:

The spirit of freedom which moved out across the world in the 1800s was primarily inspired by the fruits of freedom in the United States. The climate of free-market economics allowed science to thrive in an explosion of inventions and technical discoveries which, in merely 200 years, gave the world the gigantic new power resources of harnessed electricity, the internal combustion engine, jet propulsion, exotic space vehicles, and all the wonders of nuclear energy....."The average length of life was doubled; the quality of life was tremendously enhanced....Of course, all of this did not happen just in America, but it did flow out primarily from the swift current of freedom and prosperity which the American Founders turned loose into the spillways of human progress all over the world. In 200 years, the human race had made a 5,000-year leap."[1]

We, as Americans, have been so richly blessed. What kind of stewards will we be with that wealth for future generations?

The Founding Fathers strongly believed that our democracy could survive only if it had virtuous people at the helm. Benjamin Franklin wrote, "Only a virtuous people are capable of freedom. As nations become corrupt and vicious, they have more need of masters."[2] Throughout history, those masters have often been those who rule with tyranny and socialism.

So why should you as a Christian care about this, and how does socialism deviate from Christian values?

For a start, socialism destroys religious freedom. It destroys creativity, innovation, and ingenuity. As Bruce

Ashford puts it, "Socialism still compels many today; its vision of equality is grand. Yet untethered from a biblical framework, 'equality' becomes a weapon in the hands of an increasingly strong and frighteningly brutal state."[3]

Today, most Americans do not know the history of the death and destruction communism caused in the twentieth century. Most American college students can answer correctly when asked how many Jews died in the Holocaust. They know it is six million people because they have learned this in our schools, through popular movies, stories like *The Diary of Anne Frank*, and because of ongoing campaigns from organizations like the Victims of Communism Memorial Foundation, the Holocaust Museum, and others, who remind Americans about this history. But if you ask the average American how many victims Communism has claimed, very few would respond with the correct answer. Some sources report that it is over 100 million.[4]

According to the *2020 Report on International Religious Freedom: Venezuela*, published by the Office of International Religious Freedom at the US Department of State, "The constitution provides for freedom of religion on the condition its practice does not violate public morality, decency, or public order....There were reports that regime officials continued to prevent clergy opposing Maduro from holding religious services."[5]

Many young people today seem to be confusing socialism with social justice, even though the two are completely dissimilar. Socialism in most countries does nothing to help the poor—it often actually creates more poverty! As Sen. Rand Paul (R-KY) said, "History is replete with examples of socialism gone awry, socialism devolving into authoritarianism, genocide, and famine."[6]

To this effect, California has become a canary in the coal mine because it has fully embraced socialism and begun implementing extreme socialistic policy on the state level. It is for this reason that people are moving out of California in droves! California lost more than 117,000 residents in 2021, and about 182,000 in 2020.[7] This is not a surprise because just like in many socialistic countries, people are fleeing because of the increased government regulations and, worst of all, wealth redistribution. Recent proposed tax hikes would have increased the top tax rate on millionaires in California to an unprecedented 54 percent![8] Because of the "Green New Deal" like energy policies, California residents now pay extraordinarily high prices to power their homes and fuel their cars. Meanwhile, those same residents face massive energy shortages with blackouts and brownouts on a regular basis.

As Skousen writes, "It was in America that the Founding Fathers assembled the…ideas that produced the dynamic success formula which proved such a sensational blessing to modern man."[9] And those dynamic successes were fueled by a free-market economy that rewarded that success!

The people who fought for our country to establish the freedoms we enjoy today suffered enormous hardship. Many of them died fighting to protect our religious freedom especially. If you are a Christian, the choice that faces you is not whether you are willing to fight for what you believe. Instead, it is this: Do you want to fight right now while it may be uncomfortable and unpleasant, but you will be fighting to preserve what freedoms we already have? Or do you want to wait and fight later to regain what we had before we lost our freedom?

Long hours volunteering on a campaign, giving up a little extra money each campaign season, taking time out of your busy schedule to attend town hall meetings, and dealing with the unpleasant nature of politics pales in comparison to what people who fought in the Revolutionary War and other battles for freedom endured. Never before in our nation's history have we been so close to adopting a way of life that will eventually lead to everything we hold dear being completely stripped away. John Mackey, the founder of Whole Foods, recently stated, "Socialism has been tried 41 times in the last 100 years. Forty-one countries have tried socialism, and there have been exactly 41 failures."[10] Socialism is a political and economic system with roots in the ideas of Karl Marx. In socialism, the government owns all means of generating wealth, but individuals can own property. It is often thought of as the period between the overthrow of the capitalist system and the implementation of Communism.[11]

As one writer noted, democratic socialism is a less extreme form of socialism that puts democratic control over the economy. This, however, typically leads to the implementation of a welfare state and large increases in government regulation despite the fact that a basic capitalist system remains.[12]

Massive regulation and taxation are what socialism typically brings about regardless of what name is applied to it.

Communism is the full implementation of government control and exists when there is no class, no money, and no private ownership whatsoever. The government runs everything, and all property is communally owned.[13] All one needs to do is look at how their local US Postal Service office or their DMV operates, and then imagine that style of service applied to every single aspect of life. It is beyond imagination how anyone could think that this would improve things in our country. If the United States were a Communist country, the iPhone would most likely never have been invented because all of the government regulations and lack of incentives would most likely have stifled someone like Steve Jobs and the rest of his team's creativity.

Under free-market capitalism, there is free competition and no government regulation or interference. Entrepreneurship, hard work, and innovation are incentivized, and people are free to own property.

In China, a new model has been adopted that is unique. They have combined full-scale authoritarianism with capitalism and created what is being called a "new communism." According to historian Tomasz Kamusella, "In the wake of then Chinese leader Deng Xiaoping's 1978 reforms, a great discovery of applied politics was made in China: that you can have capitalism without democracy. Spotting a gap in the market of ideas, Deng decreed that 'to get rich is glorious,' meaning that capitalism was ideologically neutral and could serve the needs of a communist regime."[14]

Kamusella goes on to say: "The seismic shift from Soviet-style communism 1.0, based on heavy industry, to China's AI-supported communism 2.0" could mean that "civic and human rights are seriously limited and often denounced as a 'western ploy.' For instance, no individual right to vote exists in China, while the state actually owns citizens' bodies to do with them as it pleases."[15]

In America, we find this type of government control and interference shocking and unimaginable. However, conditions are ripe for Marxism to grow in this nation, according to researcher George Barna: "Previous surveys I've conducted regarding socialism and Marxism have shown that most Americans do not understand the foundations of socialism, or that socialism and Marxism are joined at the hip. The increasing rejection of basic biblical principles by adults has left an ideological vacuum that Marxism and its offshoots, such as Critical Race Theory, are seeking to fill."

Barna noted that a Marxist revolution within the United States is not as far-fetched as some people assume. "Movements that are small in the number of passionate supporters but are well-funded and adroitly execute strategic plans can transform the larger culture despite their size.

"So when it comes to the encroachment of Marxism or socialism in America, consider the situation carefully," he said. "Most Americans do not realize they support elements of Marxist ideology. A large share of the youngest adult generation—the Millennials—has positive feelings about socialism. Combine those realities with powerful and strategically placed government officials and agencies currently putting Marxist ideas into practice.

"These conditions mean that it is feasible that America could unwittingly embrace an increasing degree of Marxist principles and practices during the coming two decades."[16] In the 2020 elections, dozens of candidates endorsed by the Democratic Socialists of America (DSA) won seats all over the country, from city council to Congress. Membership in the DSA has been growing by leaps and bounds, and according to a 2019 poll, 70 percent of millennials say they would vote for a socialist.[17]

Even more shocking is a recent Yahoo News/YouGov poll that indicates "most Democrats (55%) and Republicans (53%) now believe it is 'likely' that America will 'cease to be a democracy in the future'—a stunning expression of bipartisan despair about the direction of the country. Half of all Americans (49%) express the same sentiment when independents and those who do not declare any political affiliation are factored in, while just a quarter (25%) consider the end of U.S. democracy unlikely and another quarter (25%) say they're unsure."[18]

The recent rise in socialism coming from the fringe Left should be deeply troubling to all because at its core, socialism is about replacing God with government and freedom with tyranny. America is the greatest land of opportunity the world has ever known because Americans are free to practice their own beliefs, speak their own minds, protect their own lives, pursue their own dreams, and enjoy the fruits of their own labor. Socialism directly opposes the American dream.

Advocates for socialism see Christianity as a threat and therefore believe it must be silenced, canceled, and eliminated. Socialism has been tried all over the world and has never worked, but somehow people keep getting deceived into adopting this approach. The truth is, in socialist countries, most people of faith suffer tremendously. One of the greatest ways they suffer is by having God stripped out of everything.

Pastor Mario Felix Lleonart Barroso, a Cuban refugee

and religious freedom activist, has said, "In any society, there's a close relationship between respecting religious liberty and the prosperity of other political, civic, and economic freedoms. That's why in societies where socialist, communist, or totalitarian ideologies have predominated, we see the contrary take place. Attacks on religious freedom are among the primary and most recurrent violations we see in those societies. When a nation with a democratic heritage is interrupted by a totalitarian regime that breaks the constitutional order and destroys foundational institutions, its first targets are precisely religious institutions, as well as individuals with religious beliefs."

Pastor Barroso went on to say, "Destroying the foundations of any society and guaranteeing the oppression of a population who's been stripped of its rights requires these regimes to also destroy the certainty of *Imago Dei,* the idea that we have equal dignity because we are created by God, that our rights come from Him and not from government."[19]

> *The recent rise in socialism coming from the fringe Left should be deeply troubling to all because at its core, socialism is about replacing God with government and freedom with tyranny.*

I spoke recently with my colleague and friend William J. Murray, the son of Madalyn Murray O'Hair. He made a striking statement about how "his mother made it all the way to the Supreme Court, and it cost her less than $10,000 to get there." In 1962, for less than $10,000 she had prayer removed from the schools—a decision that still impacts our country to this day. He went on to say that the primary reason that happened was because the church was not paying attention. Will we as the church do the same thing in regard to socialism and possibly lose our religious freedoms?

Right now, in America, socialism is on our doorstep. As one major donor at a fundraising event recently said to me, "My husband and I can either get involved in politics now and give away some of our money to help get the right kinds of candidates elected, or we can wait, hold on to our money, and then risk our kids having nothing to inherit. If our country gives in to full-scale socialism or Communism, the government could easily come in and just take it all!" This may sound extreme, but for anyone who remembers what happened in Cuba when Castro took power and converted them to full-scale Communism, or if you have studied places like Venezuela, there are horror stories of things just like that occurring. As Fox News reported, "Venezuela was once the wealthiest country in South America, but in recent years millions have fled the country amid mass starvation and violence after socialist policies were enacted and the government seized private industries."[20] As of December 2021, more than six million Venezuelans had left their homes, with approximately five million of them remaining in other countries in the Latin American and Caribbean regions, primarily Colombia, Peru, and Ecuador.[21]

Centuries later, the words of Irish politician John Philpot Curran still ring true: "The condition upon which God hath given liberty to man is eternal vigilance...." So the time is now! We as Christians and people who love God, love our country, and love the very things that make life precious must rise up. We must choose God over government and faith over fear. If not now, when? If not us, then who?

CHAPTER 14

GUIDANCE FOR CHURCHES AND FAITH LEADERS

I have learned over the years that when one's mind is made up, this diminishes fear. Knowing what must be done does away with fear.

—ROSA PARKS

THERE IS CONSIDERABLE misunderstanding and misinterpretation of the legal limits of the church to address political issues and candidates.

This chapter details some past important legal decisions in an effort to clarify what churches and houses of worship and/or their pastors or religious leaders may and may not do from the pulpit and as organizations. Some historical facts provide a good context for the issue as well.

In October 1801, the Connecticut Danbury Baptist Association, concerned about the protection of religious freedom, wrote a letter to President Thomas Jefferson that included the following:

> Our sentiments are uniformly on the side of religious liberty—that religion is at all times and places a matter between God and individuals—that no man ought to suffer in name, person, or effects on account of his religious opinions—that the legitimate power of civil government extends no further

than to punish the man who works ill to his neighbors; But, sir, our constitution of government is not specific.[1]

On January 1, 1802, Jefferson's response included these words:

I contemplate with sovereign reverence that act of the whole American people which declared that their legislature should "make no law respecting an establishment of religion, or prohibiting the free exercise thereof," thus building a wall of separation between Church & State. Adhering to this expression of the supreme will of the nation in behalf of the rights of conscience, I shall see with sincere satisfaction the progress those sentiments which tend to restore to man all his natural rights, convinced he has no natural right in opposition to his social duties.[2]

This was Jefferson's assurance that the federal government would never interfere with the free exercise of religion. He believed that God, not government, was the source of our rights and that the government was to be prevented from interference. His intent was not to limit religious activities in public; rather, the expectation was the limitation of the power of the government to prohibit or interfere with religious expressions.

These letters were written about a decade after the ratification of the Bill of Rights, and therefore the First Amendment. Jefferson's letter echoed ideas in the Establishment Clause, placed within that amendment. This clause remains relevant to this day. It reads: "Congress shall make no law respecting an establishment of religion or prohibiting the free exercise thereof." The government may not organize or establish a church or favor one religion over another. Jefferson was attempting to protect the church, not stifle it.

The First Amendment has two provisions regarding religion: the Establishment Clause and the Free Exercise Clause. "The Establishment Clause prohibits the government from 'establishing' a religion. The precise definition of 'establishment' is unclear. Historically, it meant prohibiting state-sponsored churches, such as the Church of England."[3]

In the 1947 case *Everson v. Board of Education*, the Supreme Court ruled as constitutional a New Jersey statute that allocated taxpayer funds to bus children to religious schools. According to the First Amendment Encyclopedia, the court determined that the statute "did not breach the 'wall of separation' between the church and state...and held that the Establishment Clause of the First Amendment applied to state and local governments as well as to the federal government."[4]

There is no doubt that the First Amendment protects the right of churches to speak on moral issues as well as to develop and circulate information on public policy matters. However, in recent years, organizations like the Freedom from Religion Foundation have sought to intimidate pastors and their congregations from getting involved in politics, especially during election seasons. Their chief tool has been the threat of a church losing its tax-exempt status under section 501(c)(3) of the Internal Revenue Code.

Unfortunately, many houses of worship and their leaders and pastors have become fearful of impacting their neighborhoods and the bigger culture via their faithful members. The law, however, actually supports pastors and churches in their mission to equip their members. Even as a nonprofit corporation, there is little a church or other type of house of worship may not legally do as long as the engagement focus is on issues, not specific candidates or political parties.

As Freedom Forum Institute so eloquently said, "The Establishment Clause separates church from state, but not religion from politics or public life." Both Thomas Jefferson and James Madison believed that there could be no real religious freedom without separating church from state. Today, the Establishment Clause prohibits all levels of government from either advancing or inhibiting religion.[5]

Nonprofit, public interest, legal, and educational organizations equipped to advocate for the legally inclusive role of churches and religious organizations have proven invaluable to fulfilling their calling and mission, and they have done so in a manner that respects the First Amendment. The nonprofit Becket (formerly the Becket Fund for Religious Liberty), for instance, states that its mission is "to protect the expression of all faiths."[6] And their clients include a broad spectrum of religious faiths. Becket observes, "Unfortunately, the rights of many religious communities are under attack, and sometimes because they stand out from the rest of society."[7] In addition, the Alliance Defending Freedom (ADF) has an entire division devoted to this called the ADF Church Alliance. More information can be found in the appendix.

Texas Values, a branch of the First Liberty Institute, another organization assisting churches with accurate legal perspectives, notes: "Many churches and pastors feel called by scripture to 'equip the saints' to represent Christ in all areas of our society, including the voting booth. Pastors should thus be supported in their goal of helping their members be good stewards in representing Christ in their civic duties."[8] A Barna poll of American voters concluded that a voter's religious faith matters in his or her voting decisions.[9] Yet civic engagement among people of faith remains limited.

Speaking about the 2016 elections, Barna stated, "There is great potential for churches and pastors to impact voting decisions. In fact, one out of every four Americans say they trust their church or pastor to exert a lot of influence on their political choices. What a tremendous opportunity for churches to position themselves as relevant to people's life choices while taking advantage of an available opportunity to influence people's lives. Our research reveals that most pastors have chosen to not speak to their congregants about the issues or the candidates....But if more pastors were willing to teach their congregants how to think biblically about political issues, matters of governance, and candidate selection, the election campaign might have been dramatically altered."[10]

Following is an overview of what churches and houses of worship can and cannot do provided in part by Liberty Institute.[11]

Churches and houses of worship may not:

- endorse or oppose a specific candidate

- contribute to or raise money for a candidate (including "in kind" contributions such as free use of church directories, use of their facilities to exclusively advantage a particular candidate, etc.)

- support or oppose legislation with more than an "insubstantial amount" of the church's annual budget, time, or activities

Churches and houses of worship may:

- register their members to vote
- distribute voters' guides if done in a nonpartisan manner
- invite candidates in a race to speak to their members and others gathered in their facility (All candidates must be invited; who and how many among those candidates accept the invitation is not the responsibility of the organization extending the invitation; it must only be equally offered. It's acceptable if only one candidate attends as long as all are invited.)
- speak about public, social, and moral issues of the day without restriction

As a private citizen, a pastor or religious leader may speak, contribute to, or volunteer for a candidate, support a member's campaign, etc. (The appendix in this book provides resources and includes additional information about the resources referenced.)

Churches may not donate to a candidate for public office; the funds with which they are entrusted are designated for "ministry" use. But church leaders and officials are allowed to speak out about issues relevant to such ministry and the values that are the foundation and/or of key importance to that ministry.

An American Center for Law and Justice document discussing churches' right to speak out on the moral issues of the day underscores the roles and freedoms of churches and houses of worship. Among other things, it makes these important points:

A. "*A primary purpose of the church is to influence the culture through advocacy of moral issues* [emphasis added]. Because every major religion promulgates a moral code, churches often speak out on the social and political issues of the day. As one commentator [Judy Ann Rosenblum] declared: 'Religion and politics have been intertwined since the birth of our nation. In a democracy created to reflect the social fabric of its citizens, religious groups have always advocated moral positions to further or impede political causes and political campaigns.'"

B. "The First Amendment protects churches' right to speak out on moral issues of the day."

C. "Under current tax law, churches may not speak out on the moral qualifications of candidates for public office. The Internal Revenue Code does not restrict churches' right to speak out on the moral and political

issues of the day, but it does prohibit
churches from speaking out on the qualifications of candidates for public office."

D."Churches may form separately incorporated
501(c)(4) organizations, which may, in turn,
form political action committees that are
free to participate in political campaigns."
(*Note that PACs do not have tax-exempt
status.*) [12]

The limitations noted are only for the church or house
of worship entity and only if the church or house of worship is a nonprofit corporation, therefore subject to relevant Internal Revenue
Service activity guidelines.
It must be noted, however,
that even though the IRS
does not mandate a 501(c)
(3) filing from churches
and houses of worship,
IRS directives are clear that the assumption is that such
religious organizations will comply with the intent and
execution of the 501(c)(3) guidelines.[13] And as long as the
leader of such organizations clearly communicates that
they are acting as a private citizen, not acting in their official capacity as leader of the church or house of worship,
there is no prohibition against active, direct political participation by that individual.

The moral commitments of any voter are protected in
the voting booth. According to the First Liberty Institute,

> *The appendix in this
> book provides resources
> and includes additional
> information about the
> resources referenced.*

"Pastors should not be intimidated from acting as pastors, calling their people to vote and giving them information so they can best represent Christ in the voting booth."[14]

If you are a pastor, consider these tools that you may use without violating your office, without compromising your message, and without derailing you from your role as a religious official and leader to be a key spokesperson for your faith.

One of the greatest problems we face in our country is the lack of civic engagement across all sectors and faiths in our pluralistic society. Yet civic engagement is part of stewarding our God-given freedoms and resources that our founders believed were the natural right of people of all faiths.

Perhaps the answer to the issue of divisive politics is focusing on things like training a new generation of leaders who will understand what is most important in the world of government. *Is it legal for a church to host a civics training?* Yes, it is legal for a church to host nonpartisan civics training.

The church and other houses of worship are the social institutions that should be catalyzing increased civic engagement in every community across America. This is our heritage. Doing more to foster civic engagement is politically neutral and will not trigger any issues with the IRS. For example, one church in Northern California is hosting a civics training using Cleon Skousen's book *The 5000 Year Leap: A Miracle That Changed the World*. A growing number of excellent resources, including websites, news magazines, online courses, and civics and history curricula, are consistent with spiritual and/or faith-specific values. Just as faith organizations embrace innovative and easily accessible resources for spiritual growth and maturity, many also have increasing interest in encouraging members to be more engaged with issues that directly affect their faith, families, and communities.

For further guidance, please look at the specific directives from the IRS website, www.irs.gov. See the drop-down section "Charities and Nonprofits," then scroll down to "Churches and Religious Organizations." The article "The Restriction of Political Campaign Intervention by Section 501(c)(3) Tax-Exempt Organizations" is most helpful.

Included in that text: "Certain activities or expenditures may not be prohibited depending on the facts and circumstances. For example, certain voter education activities (including presenting public forums and publishing voter education guides) conducted in a non-partisan manner do not constitute prohibited political campaign activity. In addition, other activities intended to encourage people to participate in the electoral process, such as voter registration and get-out-the-vote drives, would not be prohibited political campaign activity if conducted in a non-partisan manner."[15]

CHAPTER 15

THE HOPE IN GOING LOCAL

It is not the critic who counts; not the man who points out how the strong man stumbles or where the doer of deeds could have done them better. The credit belongs to the man who is actually in the arena, whose face is marred by dust and sweat and blood; who strives valiantly, who errs, who comes short again and again, because there is no effort without error and shortcoming; but who does actually strive to do the deeds; but who knows the great enthusiasms, the great devotions; who spends himself in a worthy cause; who, at the best, knows, in the end, the triumph of high achievement, and who, at the worst, if he fails, at least he fails while daring greatly, so that his place shall never be with those cold and timid souls who neither know victory nor defeat.

—THEODORE ROOSEVELT

YOU MAY BE asking, "How do I respond to my government in a biblical manner?" Luke 9:12–14 in the New King James Version tells us:

When the day began to wear away, the twelve came and said to Him, "Send the multitude away, that they may go into the surrounding towns and country, and lodge and get provisions; for we are in a deserted place here." But He said to them, "You give them something to eat." And they said, "We have no more than five loaves and two fish unless

141

we go and buy food for all these people." For there were about five thousand men. Then He said to His disciples, "Make them sit down in groups of fifty."

From this text emerge three questions that lead to action:

- Who are your twelve?
- Who is your multitude?
- What is God's plan?

In Rochester, Minnesota, seven people have been meeting for nearly four years, seeking God's will for their city and aligning their city with God's will. They are part of something called the Isaiah 9:7 Movement,[1] and they help people create apostolic teams to make a difference in their city and government. These teams are trained and then aligned with online platforms to put forth ideas about government.

Across the United States, Moms for America is hosting "Cottage Trainings," which are opportunities to get to know the principles of liberty in a powerful and engaging way. The meetings are offered online and in person.

The US Pastors Council has trained over a thousand pastors from around the country through the Institute for American Christian Citizenship. Their website also has a host of resources for pastors and average citizens looking to be more informed and is listed in the appendix section.

In Alabama, Eagle Forum has just launched a new initiative to build small groups[2] in each congressional district across the state. They are already up to eighteen small groups covering six of the seven US congressional districts.

The groups meet monthly and will be deployed as lobbyists to help impact state and federal legislation.

In Virginia, Sandy Bushue, founder of Victory in Virginia, wanted to make a difference in the governor's race. She shared at a recent meeting in Arlington, "I just thought it was extremely important—so I thought to myself, 'What can I do?' I met gubernatorial candidate Glenn Youngkin at a Prince William County event. I saw the flier for it, signed up, attended, and then I just thought, 'He's the perfect candidate!' But he was a nobody, right? Who knew Glenn Youngkin in March of 2021? And so I sent an email out to six friends who had never heard of him, and we started looking him up. And then we started having this email exchange. I added a few more friends and they all signed up to participate with get-out-the-vote efforts for the primary! So I thought, 'Well, this is interesting.' So I started sending information out, and I started getting emails back saying please add this person or that person. Eventually, I got to over 200 people!"

Bushue then began sending out information for the people on her list to copy and send out as their own email. She encouraged others to "plagiarize heavily" because she realized that she was not the influencer in this situation, her friends and acquaintances were! She then invited all of them to dinner at a restaurant the first and third Monday of every month. The dinner was Dutch treat, and she asked all of the candidates she was supporting to come and meet with these influencers and give them information to motivate them. She recruited people to serve as volunteers and help with knocking on doors. Bushue said, "I created a bunch of Indians. There were no chiefs in my organization."

She enabled and empowered average people with information she sent from her home computer and delivered via the candidates at meetings in a local restaurant. She spent almost no money and did most of the work from her kitchen table. Yet Bushue made an enormous impact on the election! Youngkin went on to defeat Democrat Terry McAuliffe in the 2021 gubernatorial race.

These are just a few examples of average people coming together to change things for the better.

One of the main things I hope you remember is that there is great hope in what can be accomplished on the local level. For instance, do you know that only 3,243 counties and their equivalents exist in the United States and its territories? That is not a huge number. If you start breaking things down to a local level, an average person can do much more than you may realize. Most people are so focused on what is happening in areas they can't control (like the conflicts and gridlock in Washington, the border crisis, the overall economy, etc.) that they fail to see the incredible impact they can have on areas they *can* influence or control (like local education decisions, getting involved in local or even statewide campaigns, or running for local offices like school board or county clerk).

You can also start shopping with your values and be more strategic about your purchases so that you avoid supporting companies focused primarily on liberal social agendas. Voting with your wallet means supporting the right candidates, but it can also mean supporting the right companies. In the appendix, I have included information about organizations that can help you do this and that will give you tools to make wiser shopping decisions.

The reality is, in the United States, we don't have just *one* election for US president, we really have fifty state elections. And each state has a different process controlled by the county and city election officials—which makes local politics all the more important. In California, for instance, a voter can show up at their

> There is great hope in what can be accomplished on the local level.

polling location without any documents and still vote. In Wisconsin, however, you will have to show a valid photo ID to vote. In Connecticut, a voter will be asked for an identification card at their local polling place, but if they do not have one, they can still vote (for certain first-time voters, this will be a provisional ballot that will be resolved at a later date). And in Arizona, to vote you must substantiate your identity, but you can use two forms of ID that don't have a photo.[3] This is why local politics is so incredibly important. Your county and city officials have a lot of power, and they can make a huge impact.

When I worked on Capitol Hill, a lobbyist remarked to me that she was nice to everyone, even the most junior staffers in a congressional office, because, as she put it, "Little staffers grow up to be big staffers!" The same is true with local politicians. Some of them will eventually go on to run for higher and higher offices, and one day they may even run for president. Yet we often overlook this aspect of our system and rarely pay attention to whom we are grooming to serve as the future leaders on the bigger stages. Many people don't even vote in local elections! Low-voter turnout plagues local government elections all across the country. According to the *New York Times*, "Across the U.S., only 15 to 27 percent of eligible voters cast a ballot in their local election."⁴

Local leaders can also have an enormous impact on the class and racial divides that our nation is facing in epic proportion. Often, the faith community is the most effective at healing and uniting people. At a time when the division in our country is running rampant, we must choose leaders who will truly demonstrate integrity and work with the faith community to solve problems. Who better to work with that community than someone they know and trust?

What does a homegrown citizen movement look like? The first step is to create an information network that allows diverse and geographically dispersed concerned citizens to communicate and share knowledge with each other. A few thoughts to consider:

- Have a strategy. Pick one office or issue you want to change on the local level.

- Realize that sometimes it can take years to prevail, so recruit a group of committed core leaders who will remain involved for the long haul.

- Attend public meetings! This is where you start to learn the players and the issues. Many of these meetings occur monthly. Because of the coronavirus, many of them are now allowing people to attend online. School board/PTA, city/county council, and zoning board meetings are just a few examples of meetings to consider attending.

- Actively recruit ethical candidates, and be on the lookout for people of integrity who would be willing to run so they could be ready to enter the race if a current elected official retires or runs for another office. Never let a less than desirable candidate run unopposed.

- One way to recruit and credential candidates is to appoint them to local boards and commissions (planning, emergency service, parks and recreation, etc.). Serving on these panels is a way to learn about government processes, running meetings in government settings, public speaking, and messaging.

- Remember that losses are inevitable. Count them as a learning experience and regroup. Good candidates and good issues will live to win another day.

- Combine technology (social media) with traditional actions (door to door).

- Money matters, but mobilizing volunteers and igniting "fervor" among your supporters matters as well.

- Deliver on your promises. Voters want change. Give it to them. Have a well-developed plan that you will execute once your candidate is elected.

- Go to Runforoffice.org and look at what will be voted on in the next election. If you see a position that you might want to run for, find out who now occupies it and go meet with them! Have coffee and get to know them. If they align with your values, help them on their next campaign. This will help you learn and prepare you to run your own campaign in the future!

- Once you get to know a candidate, ask if they plan to run again for re-election. Sometimes people are ready to let someone else take their spot if they can find someone they can trust to endorse for that office. But you won't know unless you get to know them and then ask!

- Push for more investigative journalism by local papers. Because so many newspapers have had to scale back due to the rise of social media, etc., many have had to quit paying for investigative journalists. This is a crucial check and balance in our system that is being eliminated more and more. Consider working with other community leaders to find ways to foster this and bring it back.

These are just some of the ways you can make a difference. Another step to turning the tide in our fight to preserve freedom and restore integrity is to learn the laws. Push for sunshine laws, open meeting laws, and adequate public notice laws if more need to be in place. Know your options to go to the courts if you lose a vote in a public forum. Average citizens who are trained and do their homework can often be just as effective as attorneys because they are passionate and know what is at stake. But if all we do is sit back and leave things to someone else, we will lose every time.

Professor Arthur Brooks suggests, "Find a way to bring politics more into your sphere of influence so it no longer qualifies as an external locus of control. Simply clicking through angry political Facebook posts by people with whom you already agree will most likely worsen your mood and help no one. Instead, get involved in a tangible way—volunteering, donating money or even running for office. This transforms you from victim of political circumstance to problem solver."[5]

CHAPTER 16

GOD OVER GOVERNMENT

Send your good men into the ministry, but
send your best men into politics.

—CHAPLAIN JAMES FORD

A FASCINATING DISCOVERY HAS taken place recently in the state of California. Locals there attest that the wildfires that have ravaged the landscape, lives, and livelihoods of residents for a decade don't seem to be getting any better. They seem to be getting worse, more frequent, and more devastating.

The key question at hand is: How do you decrease wildfires in a largely arid landscape that gets more vulnerable with every fire? The answer: goats. No kidding. What Californians and residents in many other Western states have discovered is that when herds of goats are set free to graze in a dry landscape that is prone to wildfire, they feed on the invasive species of weeds and plants that come up after land has been scorched or not properly stewarded. In a short period of time, these herds can clean up acres upon acres in a manner more thorough and efficient than any machinery or chemical treatment. It's a picture of what can happen in America when we come together as a herd on common ground.

When we agree that we are done with the wildfires that have scorched our great land and set out together to clear the weeds and invading species, we will not only diminish the rate of wildfires, we will also restore what is beautiful in the land and what is native—the foundational values on which this country was founded.

If you are ready to put a stop to the corruption, the erosion of freedom, and the extreme division that have become so common in our political system, I pray this book will be an inspiration and a reference guide.

Just steps from the US Capitol, carved into the white granite walls of Union Station, the timeless words of James Russell Lowell often go unnoticed by the hundreds of people who hurry beneath them each day rushing to catch a train:

> Be noble! and the nobleness that
> Lies in other men—sleeping but
> Never dead—will rise in majesty
> To meet thine own.[1]

In the mid-nineties, while working as a Hill staffer, I often attended prayer meetings and Bible studies held in the congressional office buildings. I frequently heard then House chaplain James D. Ford say, "Send your good men into the ministry; send your best men into politics." I'm here to tell you that means women too. Do not be fooled into thinking that if you are building a career or raising a family, you are somehow exempt from an active role in your government or in supporting those in it.

We all have gifts to share, and we are modeling behavior for the next generation, whether that is for our own children or the young people we encounter in our community or work environment. The next generation is watching us. Will they emulate our good works or blame us for leaving them a society that is a tragic mess? In his novel *The Power of One*, Bryce Courtenay contended that the actions of one person can impact the entire world. *Will you have an impact?*

I have hope for our country and our world, and I have hope that you will join me, one step at a time, one voice at a time, in this critical moment in our nation's history.

Be willing to go out and trust God! Remember, an individual *can* make a difference. Consider these practical steps you can take immediately. The following list offers some suggestions that will fit every personality and calling within the body of Christ. This list is not meant to overwhelm you, just to give you a variety of options for ways to get involved. Pray about what God would have YOU to do personally.

Steps You Can Take to Get Started Today

1. **Pray and fast.**

2. **Vote.** Many Christians are registered but don't vote! If *every* Christian voted faithfully, we would win most of the races.

3. **Get involved in primaries**, not just general elections. *Everyone* needs to be doing something to help good candidates. This is critically important to weed out the good candidates from the mediocre or the bad.

4. **Do your homework** on who you are voting for—treat it like a job interview, not a passive activity. Listen to interviews with candidates and officeholders. There is often more veracity in radio than in other media because you get everything "straight from the horse's mouth," so to speak.

5. **Give money** directly to good candidates.

6. **Ask God if *you* are being called to run** for office in your community. Consider running for the school board or county clerk. These positions are essential to the community. County clerks oversee all election processes and procedures. The primary function of the school board is to oversee the education of students in the community.

7. **Recruit a good support team** of those in your community who can provide financial backing as well as influence, then recruit good candidates to run with the backing of that team to support them.

8. **Get trained.** Learn the power of connection and storytelling to help get your point across when speaking out on issues in your community or state.

9. **Get informed.** Be very discerning about the sources of your news. Stay on top of what is happening and keep up with current information. Ignore the temptation to turn off

the news. Instead of letting all the problems
you see overwhelm you, pray and choose
one thing you are passionate about and
focus on making a difference there. Follow
local as well as national news.

10. **Go door-to-door** for your candidate! A
study conducted by two Ivy League college professors, Alan Gerber and Donald
Green, shows that one of the most effective
ways to reach voters amid all the noise of
impersonal TV ads and social media is still
the personal touch of going door-to-door.[2]
Candidates who don't have money to pay
people to do this need good volunteers to
help. This is one of the most highly effective
and efficient ways to make a difference for
your candidate and to turn out voters.

11. **Volunteer to be a poll worker** or poll
watcher during the next election. Volunteer
to work on a campaign.

12. **Support political leaders** who are aligned
with your values. Write letters to the editor,
throw a fundraiser, call into radio and television talk shows, and speak up about your
candidate to get their name out there.

13. **Get to know the staff** that work for the
candidate or elected official. Full-time
staff members usually control the flow of

information available to legislators and other elected officials.

14. **Utilize "amplification" techniques.** When a good candidate or elected official makes a key point that you support, repeat it on social media or call your local radio show and give credit to that person. This helps others recognize them and gives them more "earned" media (media they don't have to pay for). We need to echo and support each other.

15. **Take civics training.** Make sure you and your children receive high-quality civics education.

16. **Encourage young people to apply for internships.** Help them get involved more directly in government by seeking internships with good leaders, and encourage them to participate in Youth Legislature events and programs like TeenPact, Turning Point USA, Young Americans for Liberty (YAL), the YMCA Youth and Government (YAG) program, and Summit Ministries Christian Worldwide trainings.

17. **Stop giving your money** to the companies and people who are not in line with your values—shop smarter, shop local. Check out organizations like 2nd Vote, Stop Corporate Tyranny, and the National Center for Public Policy Research's Free Enterprise Project.

18. **Consider getting appointed** to a board or a commission. Talk with your governor's appointments secretary about serving in this way.

19. **Utilize social media**, but do it strategically. Remember, Facebook is not a Dear Diary, it's a digital newsletter. Be strategic with what you post. Build a social media presence, and use other mediums (like email or platforms where you own your data) to prevent social media companies from influencing or controlling what you communicate. When a candidate places an ad, they depend on citizens like *you* to like and share those posts. This can make a big difference for a candidate in a close election. By just "liking" and sharing your favorite candidates with your friends on Facebook and Twitter, you can change the trajectory of a campaign without ever leaving the comfort of your home.

20. **Realize that you have influence**, and don't be afraid to use it. It may be two people, or it may be two million, but influence who you can to participate more actively in our political processes.

Once you have explored your options to make an impact as an individual, think about joining others to increase your reach. Think about the audience you want to impress. What do you want them to do once you connect with them? Start with the end in mind, then find others in your community to partner with to accomplish your goals. Link up with a group of people who think like you to sustain you. Then, once you link up, strategize about how to make a difference in your community, county, or state.

For those who are brave enough to step directly into the arena, four elements seem to be needed to succeed in running for office. Two of them are the responsibility of the individual, and the other two fall under the body of Christ as a whole. For the individual, first and foremost, you must know that you are called to serve on the mountain of government. Once you know that, you will also need to be trained. You may feel like David facing Goliath at times, but David was so successful because he was trained!

In his book *Redeeming Work*, Bryan J. Dik wrote, "Goliath sized David up as 'little more than a boy' (1 Sam. 17:42), but that boy had already killed at least two of the fiercest wild animals who walked the earth and did so by grabbing their fur and beating them to death (1 Sam. 17:34–37). Most likely, David had also developed lethal aim with his sling. He would soon go on to become a high-ranking army official, earning recognition for slaying 'tens of thousands' (1 Sam. 18:7). And while David defeated Goliath because David invited God to work through him, there is no indication that God superseded David's gifts as he did so; as far as we can tell, God worked through them."[3]

The third critically necessary element for candidates is financial backing. Without this, it is almost impossible to succeed in most cases. However, as we have seen with many candidates who self-fund and then do not win, this on its own is simply not enough to achieve victory a majority of the time. The fourth element, support, must be present as well. We as people of faith have a responsibility, financially and with our influence and time, to support those who are called and trained.

This book is my effort to give you tools as well as knowledge to understand that there is *hope*, to know that all is not lost and it is not too late to preserve our freedoms. There are good and noble people in government fighting for what is right; they just need more support and reinforcements from people like you. We are "one nation under God," and that is what makes us indivisible. When we allow ourselves to be divided, that puts us at risk of being one nation under government, not under God.

President Donald Trump said it best at a veterans' event at the Kennedy Center in July 2017: "And above all else we know this: *In America, we don't worship government, we worship God*" (emphasis added).[4]

So if that is what you believe, I am asking you to join me. Let's start a movement to keep God first in our nation, a movement about choosing God over government and not allowing government to replace God.

> There are good and noble people in government fighting for what is right; they just need more support and reinforcements from people like you.

I invite you to reach out to me at Godovergovernment. com, where you can sign up for more information and resources. You can also go there to subscribe to my podcast, *Running Into the Fire*.

This is truly a time for heroes. It is a time for people to stand up and be counted. In the same way that children do not raise themselves and healthy gardens do not stay free of weeds on their own, a nation does not stay strong without the care of its people. It is time that we take full responsibility for what we have been entrusted to steward. Let's stop focusing only on what is wrong. Let's appreciate what is right. There's greatness in the people that make up this country, and there's greatness in you. So rise up! Your country needs you. Fortune favors the bold, but more importantly, God honors and exalts His faithful ones.

With God's help, I believe we can change our government and our nation for the better. It's time for the body of Christ to step into its own power.

APPENDIX

RESOURCES ON RUNNING FOR OFFICE

- Run for Office (https://www.runforoffice.org/) offers tools and even a free online course.

- The Secretary of State website in your home state can offer election and filing information as well as data on previous campaigns and how much the candidates spent. This will give you some idea of how much you need to raise.

- State Republican and Democratic party websites also provide election information, filing deadlines, resources, events, and other resources.

TRAINING RESOURCES FOR CHRISTIANS WHO WANT TO RUN FOR OFFICE OR GET INVOLVED IN POLITICS

- Leadership Institute: https://leadershipinstitute.org

- Kingdom in Politics: https://www.kingdominpolitics.com/

- Family Policy Alliance: https://familypolicyalliance.com/ statesmen-academy/about

- The Policy Circle: https://www.thepolicycircle.org

- Isaiah 9:7 Project: www.Isaiah97.com

- The D. James Kennedy Center for Christian Leadership: https://www.statesman.org

- Wilberforce Alliance: https://www.wilberforcealliance.com

- Leadership Institute's "School Board Campaign Training": https://www.leadershipinstitute.training/courses/school-board

- Leadership Institute's "Door-to-Door Campaigning" (training guide): https://www.leadershipinstitute.org/guide/DoortoDoor.pdf

- The Great Awakening Project: https://gapmovement.com

- LBJ Women's Campaign School at the University of Texas at Austin's Lyndon B. Johnson School of Public Affairs: https://lbjwcs.lbj.utexas.edu

- Republican National Convention Political Education: https://gop.com/political-education

- Democratic National Committee activist and volunteer training: https://democrats.org/take-action/trainings

- Christians Engaged:
  https://christiansengaged.org

- Foundations of Freedom:
  https://www.foundationsoffreedom.com

- American Renewal Project:
  https://theamericanrenewalproject.org

- Article by Ken Sande, author of *The Peacemaker*, about relational wisdom:
  https://rw360.org/2020/10/22/politics-as-ministry2/https://rw360.org/2018/03/05/politics-pride-and-emotion-2

RESOURCES FOR MAKING WISE SHOPPING CHOICES

- Stop Corporate Tyranny:
  https://stopcorporatetyranny.org

- 2ndVote: www.2ndvote.org

- The National Center for Public Policy Research: https://nationalcenter.org/programs/free-enterprise-project

CIVICS TRAINING ORGANIZATIONS

- Constituting America:
  https://constitutingamerica.org

- The Policy Circle:
  https://www.thepolicycircle.org/cler

- The Dreyfuss Civics Initiative:
  https://thedreyfussinitiative.org

- Citizen University: https://citizenuniversity.us

- Prager University: https://www.prageru.com

- Freedom Civics: https://freedomcivics.org

- Hillsdale College's 1776 Curriculum:
  https://k12.hillsdale.edu/Curriculum/
  The-Hillsdale-1776-Curriculum

- National Civic League:
  https://www.nationalcivicleague.org/
  resource-center

- Bill of Rights Institute:
  https://billofrightsinstitute.org

- Center for Christian Civics:
  https://www.christiancivics.org

POLITICAL TRAINING FOR YOUNG LEADERS

- TeenPact: https://teenpact.com

- Turning Point USA: https://www.tpusa.com/

- Young Americans for Liberty: https://
  yaliberty.org/

- YMCA Youth and Government: https://www.
  ymcayag.org/

- Forge Leadership Network: https://
  forgeleadership.org

- Generation Joshua:
  https://generationjoshua.org

- Summit Ministries: https://www.summit.org

RESOURCES FOR INTERNSHIPS

- Leadership Institute:
  https://www.leadershipinstitute.org/training/
  Schools

- The Heritage Foundation: https://www.
  heritage.org/young-leaders-program/
  departments-and-intern-roles

- US House of Representatives employment
  bulletin: https://www.house.gov/employment/
  positions-with-members-and-committees/
  subscribe-to-the-house-employment-bulletin

- US Senate internships: https://www.senate.
  gov/employment/po/internships.htm

- Congressional Committee
  internships: https://www.house.gov/
  educators-and-students/college-internships

- Roll Call's "Ultimate Capitol Hill Internship
  Guide": https://rollcall.com/2014/07/13/
  ultimate-capitol-hill-internship-guide-
  getting-a-job

Resources on Church and State Issues

- The IRS: https://www.irs.gov/pub/irs-news/fs-06-17.pdf

- American Center for Law & Justice: https://aclj.org/free-speech-2/churches-free-speech-and-the-regulations-of-the-irs-regarding-elections-2004

- Alliance Defending Freedom (ADF): https://adflegal.org/

  - ADF's "Pastors, Churches & Politics: 5 Things to Know" explains the laws surrounding tax-exempt status and how they affect churches' political engagement: https://www.adfchurchalliance.org/electionguide

  - ADF's "A Legal Guide for Churches: Five Things to Know": https://wpsmc.adflegal.org/wp-content/uploads/2020/02/adf_election2020_FINAL.pdf

  - ADF's "Living Your Faith in the Public Square": https://adflegal.org/issues/religious-freedom/public-square

  - ADF's "Defending Religious Freedom": https://adflegal.org/issues/religious-freedom/church

  - ADF's Church Alliance: www.adfchurchalliance.org

- Legal help for Christian ministries: https://www.adfministryalliance.org/

- First Liberty Institute's "Religious Liberty Protection Kit": https://firstliberty.org/wp-content/uploads/2021/11/Religious-Liberty-Protection-Kit-for-Houses-of-Worship-PDF.pdf

- "Church & Government: Know Your Legal Rights": https://firstliberty.org/wp-content/uploads/2016/04/Know_your-rights_handout_CHURCH11.pdf

Resources on Election Integrity

- Election Integrity Network: https://whoscounting.us/
  - Election Integrity Network's "Citizens Guide": https://whoscounting.us/citizensguide/
  - Election Integrity Network's latest resources: https://whoscounting.us/resources/
  - Election Integrity Network's "Facts and Views About the Left's Planned Federal Takeover of America's Election Systems": https://whoscounting.us/wp-content/uploads/2021/09/EIN-Messaging-Fact-Sheet-and-Polling-Data-on-Federal-Takeover-of-Elections-HR-4.pdf

- True the Vote: https://www.truethevote.org/

- Transparency International (a resource showing how other countries have worked to stop election corruption): https://www.transparency.org/en/

Resources From the Congressional Management Foundation

- "Communicating with Congress": https://www.congressfoundation.org/projects/communicating-with-congress

- "Building Relationships with Members: How to Thrive in the Small Village of Congress": https://www.congressfoundation.org/news/blog/1586

Voter Guides and Resources for Researching Candidates

- Transparency USA: https://www.transparencyusa.org/

- iVoterGuide: https://ivoterguide.com/

- Ballotpedia: www.Ballotpedia.org

- My Faith Votes: https://www.myfaithvotes.org/

- Faith Wins: https://faithwins.us/

- Family Policy Alliance: https://familypolicyalliance.com/

- Faith and Freedom Coalition:
  https://www.ffcoalition.com/

- Eagle Forum: https://eagleforum.org/

Guidance on PACs

- How to set up a super PAC:
  https://www.venable.com/
  insights/publications/2016/05/
  setting-up-and-operating-a-super-pac

- Federal Election Commission guidance on
  the types of PACs: https://www.fec.gov/help-
  candidates-and-committees/registering-pac/
  types-nonconnected-pacs/

- National Conference of State Legislatures'
  state PAC contribution limits:
  https://www.ncsl.org/Portals/1/Documents/
  Elections/Contribution_Limits_to_
  Candidates_2020_2021.pdf

- FEC guidance on giving limits:
  https://www.fec.gov/introduction-campaign-
  finance/understanding-ways-support-
  federal-candidates/

Resource on Socialism

- Competitive Enterprise Institute:
  https://cei.org/issues/capitalism/
  capitalism-and-free-enterprise/

- Victims of Communism Memorial Foundation: https://victimsofcommunism.org/about/

RECOMMENDED READING

- *The 5000 Year Leap: A Miracle That Changed the World* by W. Cleon Skousen

- *Losing Freedom: Socialism and the Growing Threat to American Life, Liberty and Free Enterprise* by Linden Blue (This is one of the best books on socialism out there. Every high school student should be required to read this.)

- *Right to Petition: A Practical Guide to Creating Change in Government with Political Advocacy Tools and Tips* by Nicole Tisdale

- *Well Versed: Biblical Answers to Today's Tough Issues* by James L. Garlow

- *The Righteous Fight: Reclaiming the Soul of America* by Stephanie Maier

- *Local Politics Matters: A Citizen's Guide to Making a Difference* by Richard J. Meagher, PhD

ABOUT THE AUTHOR

TERRI HASDORFF IS a former congressional candidate with more than twenty years of experience working at the intersection of faith and politics. She began her career in the White House Office of Public Liaison, where she had the honor of working with faith leaders from across the country.

She then served on Capitol Hill for six years. Her most meaningful assignments focused on two things: bringing accountability and transparency to government and pushing back discrimination against faith-based organizations on the front lines of fighting poverty. Hasdorff was selected by the governor of Alabama to build the first Office of Faith-Based and Community Initiatives for the state, which brought resources and grant opportunities to nonprofits and faith-based organizations across Alabama. The White House recognized the office as a model for other states to replicate. In 2006, the White House appointed her to serve as the director of the United States Agency for International Development's Center for Faith-Based and Community Initiatives, focusing on America's efforts to empower the world's poorest people through partnering with grassroots poverty fighters.

In addition, Hasdorff has extensive experience with fundraising, political campaign management, and managing a federal super PAC. She earned a bachelor's degree from Samford University, is a graduate of the Senior Executives in State and Local Government program at the John F. Kennedy School of Government at Harvard University, and is currently completing a master's in business administration at Oxford University.

NOTES

INTRODUCTION

1. Lois Beckett, "US Records Largest Annual Increase in Murders in Six Decades," Guardian, September 27, 2021, https://www.theguardian.com/us-news/2021/sep/27/us-murder-rate-increase-2020.

2. "Overdose Death Rates," National Institute on Drug Abuse, January 20, 2022, https://nida.nih.gov/research-topics/trends-statistics/overdose-death-rates.

3. "United States Profile," Prison Policy Initiative, accessed June 15, 2022, https://www.prisonpolicy.org/profiles/US.html.

4. "Incarceration Rates by Country 2022," World Population Review, accessed June 6, 2022, https://worldpopulationreview.com/country-rankings/incarceration-rates-by-country.

5. Tim Morris, "The Most Corrupt State? Louisiana Owns It: Opinion," NOLA.com, July 22, 2019, https://www.nola.com/opinions/article_37b5e0eb-0a70-5f20-8863-3e90d00e7357.html.

6. Gordon Russell and John Simerman, "Ex-New Orleans Mayor Ray Nagin, Due for 2023 Release, Sent Home Early Due to Coronavirus," NOLA.com, April 27, 2020, https://www.nola.com/news/courts/article_2535b506-88f2-11ea-bf51-071512b52215.html.

7. Bill Chappell, "Former Rep. 'Duke' Cunningham Freed After Bribery Sentence," NPR, June 4, 2013, https://www.npr.org/sections/thetwo-way/2013/06/04/188667106/former-rep-duke-cunningham-freed-after-bribery-sentence.

8. Dave Bartkowiak Jr., "Nearly 8 Years Ago: Kwame Kilpatrick Is Convicted on 24 Federal Felony Counts," Click on Detroit, accessed June 6, 2022, https://www. clickondetroit.com/news/local/2021/01/20/nearly-8-years-ago-kwame-kilpatrick-is-convicted-on-24-federal-felony-counts/.

9. Beth Cann, "Former Alabama House Speaker Mike Hubbard Will Not Have Radio Station Licenses Revoked," Alabama Today, May 11, 2022, https://altoday.com/ archives/45376-former-alabama-house-speaker-mike-hubbard-will-not-have-radio-station-licenses-revoked.

10. Coronavirus Resource Center, Johns Hopkins University and Medicine, accessed June 6, 2022, https://coronavirus. jhu.edu/map.html.

11. Tereza Pultarova, "The Devastating Wildfires of 2021 Are Breaking Records and Satellites Are Tracking It All," Space.com, August 11, 2021, https://www.space. com/2021-record-wildfire-season-from-space.

12. Tracy Munsil, "CRC Report Finds Nearly 70% of Americans Claim to be 'Christian,' But What Does That Mean?" Arizona Christian University, August 31, 2021, https://www.arizonachristian.edu/2021/08/31/crc-report-finds-nearly-70-of-americans-claim-to-be-christian-but-what-does-that-mean/.

13. John Gramlich, "What the 2020 Electorate Looks Like by Party, Race and Ethnicity, Age, Education and Religion," Pew Research Center, October 26, 2020, https://www. pewresearch.org/fact-tank/2020/10/26/what-the-2020-electorate-looks-like-by-party-race-and-ethnicity-age-education-and-religion/.

14. Kendall Breitman, "Poll: Majority of Millennials Can't Name a Senator From Their Home State," Politico, February 3, 2015, https://www.politico.com/ story/2015/02/poll-millennials-state-senators-114867.

15. "Americans' Knowledge of the Branches of Government Is Declining," Annenberg Public Policy Center of the

University of Pennsylvania, September 13, 2016, https://www.annenbergpublicpolicycenter.org/americans-knowledge-of-the-branches-of-government-is-declining/.

16. John Schwartz, "How to Fight a Wildfire: Grueling Work and Managing Risks," *New York Times*, September 15, 2020, https://www.nytimes.com/2020/09/15/climate/firefighting-techniques.html.

CHAPTER 1

1. "Mathare Valley," Bridge Ministries, accessed June 6, 2022, http://bridge-ministries.net/mathare-valley/.
2. "Mathare Valley," Bridge Ministries.

CHAPTER 2

1. I made this point during my testimony before the Committee on International Relations regarding the role of faith-based organizations in US programming in Africa. See Committee on International Relations, House of Representatives, 109th Congress, *The Role of Faith-Based Organizations in United States Programming in Africa* (Washington, DC: U.S. Government Printing Office, 2006), 10.
2. Katherine Huggins, "Candidates Poured Over $100 Million of Their Own Cash Into Campaigns in 2021," OpenSecrets, March 15, 2022, https://www.opensecrets.org/news/2022/03/congressional-candidates-poured-nearly-100-million-of-their-own-cash-into-campaigns-in-2021/.
3. "Top Self-Funding Candidates," OpenSecrets, accessed June 6, 2022, https://www.opensecrets.org/elections-overview/top-self-funders.
4. Brandon Showalter, "Facebook Shuts Down Christian Ministry's Page With No Explanation," Christian Post, October 8, 2020, https://www.christianpost.com/news/facebook-shuts-down-christian-ministrys-page-with-no-explanation.html.

5. Michelle C. Danko, "Christian University Prof Suspended From Facebook," Faith Filled Family Magazine, January 28, 2021, https://faithfilledfamily. com/christian-university-professor-banned-facebook/.

Chapter 3

1. Committee on International Relations, House of Representatives, 109th Congress, *The Role of Faith-Based Organizations in United States Programming in Africa*.

2. Carey Nieuwhof, "A Response to Christians Who Are Done With Church," Carey Nieuwhof, https:// careynieuwhof.com/a-response-to-christians-who-are-done-with-church/.

3. Magdalena Martinez and Anna Dulaney, *Religious-Based Initiatives*, AIDSCAP/Family Health International, 1997, https://pdf.usaid.gov/pdf_docs/pnacf550.pdf.

4. Rick Warren, "8 Reasons the Church Is the Greatest Force on Earth," ChurchLeaders, July 6, 2016, https:// churchleaders.com/outreach-missions/outreach-missions-articles/282315-reasons-church-greatest-force-earth-rick-warren-outreach.html.

5. "Active Conservative Christians Were Huge for Trump SAGE Con Turnout and Trump Vote Set Records," Arizona Christian University Cultural Research Center, November 24, 2020, https://www.arizonachristian. edu/wp-content/uploads/2020/11/CRC_FRC-SAGE_ ConSurvey_Digital_01_20201124.pdf.

6. "Born Again Christians Were a Significant Factor in President Bush's Re-Election," Barna Group, November 9, 2004, https://www.barna.com/research/born-again-christians-were-a-significant-factor-in-president-bushs-re-election/.

7. "From John Adams to Massachusetts Militia, 11 October 1798," National Archives, accessed June 6, 2022, https:// founders.archives.gov/documents/Adams/99-02-02-3102.

8. Arthur C. Brooks, "Religious Faith and Charitable Giving," *Policy Review*, October 1, 2003, https://www.hoover.org/research/religious-faith-and-charitable-giving.

CHAPTER 4

1. James Dean, "Fear Year: Pandemic Politics Made Us Anxious, but Hardly Safer," Cornell Chronicle, April 15, 2021, https://news.cornell.edu/stories/2021/04/fear-year-pandemic-politics-made-us-anxious-hardly-safer.

2. *Oxford English Dictionary*, 2nd ed., s.v. "pestilence (n.,b.2)," https://www.oed.com/oed2/00176574#.

3. *Oxford English Dictionary*, s.v. "politics," as quoted in Brian Lund, *Housing Politics in the United Kingdom* (Bristol, UK: Policy Press, 2016), 2.

4. De La Salle College of Saint Benilde, "UNDSELF_Politics-Theory of Authority," Course Hero, https://www.coursehero.com/file/105672120/UNDSELF-Politics-Theory-of-Authoritypdf/.

5. "Lord Acton Quote Archive," Acton Institute, accessed June 6, 2022, https://www.acton.org/research/lord-acton-quote-archive.

6. Loren Cunningham, *Making Jesus Lord* (Seattle, WA: YWAM Publishing, 1989), Kindle location 1661.

CHAPTER 5

1. Rose Lagacé, "The Devil Wears Prada Cerulean Sweater Monologue," *Art Departmental* (blog), July 17, 2017, https://artdepartmental.com/blog/devil-wears-prada-cerulean-monologue/https://artdepartmental.com/blog/devil-wears-prada-cerulean-monologue/.

2. Lagacé, "The Devil Wears Prada Cerulean Sweater Monologue."

3. Charles Hunt and Casey Burgat, "The Who, What, When, Where, and Why of Congressional Campaign Spending," LegBranch.org, September 25, 2018, https://www.legbranch.org/2018-9-20-the-who-what-when-where-and-why-of-congressional-campaign-spending/.

4. Lata Nott, "Political Advertising on Social Media Platforms," *Human Rights* 45, no. 3 (June 25, 2020), https://www.americanbar.org/groups/crsj/publications/human_rights_magazine_home/voting-in-2020/political-advertising-on-social-media-platforms/.

5. Herb Jackson, "A Year Out, Political Groups Prepare For What Could Be the Most Expensive Midterms Ever," *Roll Call*, November 1, 2021, https://rollcall.com/2021/11/01/a-year-out-outside-political-groups-prepare-for-potentially-costliest-midterms/.

6. Nott, "Political Advertising on Social Media Platforms."

7. "Did Money Win?" OpenSecrets, accessed June 3, 2022, https://www.opensecrets.org/elections-overview/winning-vs-spending?cycle=2020.

Chapter 6

1. Adam McCann, "Most & Least Politically Engaged States," WalletHub, October 13, 2020, https://wallethub.com/edu/most-least-politically-engaged-states/7782.

2. Aaron Blake, "New York, Andrew Cuomo, and the Six Most Corrupt States in the Country," *Washington Post*, August 11, 2021, https://www.washingtonpost.com/politics/2021/08/11/six-most-corrupt-states/.

3. Michael Lipka and Benjamin Wormald, "How Religious Is Your State?" Pew Research Center, February 29, 2016, https://www.pewresearch.org/fact-tank/2016/02/29/how-religious-is-your-state/?state=alabama.

4. Megan Brenan, "Satisfaction With U.S. Dips; Biden Approval Steady at 41%," Gallup, May 24, 2022, https://news.gallup.com/poll/393038/satisfaction-dips-biden-approval-steady.aspx; Adam Schrader, "76% of Americans Disapprove of Congress' Performance," UPI, April 1, 2022, https://www.upi.com/Top_News/US/2022/04/01/gallup-poll-76-percent-americans-disapprove-congress/8461648857738/.

5. *Merriam-Webster*, s.v. "maven," accessed June 16, 2022, https://www.merriam-webster.com/dictionary/maven.

6. "Voter Turnout," MIT Election Data and Science Lab, accessed June 16, 2022, https://electionlab.mit.edu/ research/voter-turnout; Amelia Thomson-DeVeaux, Jasmine Mithani, and Laura Bronner, "Why Many Americans Don't Vote," FiveThirtyEight, October 26, 2020, https://projects.fivethirtyeight.com/non-voters-poll-2020-election/.

7. John Gramlich, "What the 2020 Electorate Looks Like by Party, Race and Ethnicity, Age, Education and Religion," Pew Research Center, October 26, 2020, https://www. pewresearch.org/fact-tank/2020/10/26/what-the-2020-electorate-looks-like-by-party-race-and-ethnicity-age-education-and-religion/.

8. "2012: What's at Stake?" Family Research Council, accessed June 3, 2022, https://downloads.frcaction.org/ EF/EF12B17.pdf.

9. "Voter Turnout," MIT Election Data and Science Lab.

CHAPTER 7

1. "Donor Demographics," OpenSecrets, accessed June 4, 2022, https://www.opensecrets.org/elections-overview/ donor-demographics.

2. "Donor Demographics," OpenSecrets.

3. "The American Religious Landscape in 2020," Public Religion Research Institute, July 6, 2021, https://www. prri.org/research/2020-census-of-american-religion/.

4. Haleluya Hadero and Associated Press, "Americans Gave a Record $471 Billion to Charity in 2020," *Fortune*, June 15, 2021, https://fortune.com/2021/06/15/americans-gave-a-record-471-billion-to-charity-in-2020-pandemic/.

5. James M. Ferris, "A Generation of Impact: The Evolution of Philanthropy Over the Past 25 Years," Center on Philanthropy and Public Policy, March 2021, https://cppp. usc.edu/wp-content/uploads/2021/03/A-Generation-of-Impact.pdf.

6. "Record Setting 5 Billion Political Texts Sent In October," PR Newswire, November 2, 2020, https://www.

prnewswire.com/news-releases/record-setting-5-billion-political-texts-sent-in-october-2020-301165329.html.

7. "Do Messaging Speeds Matter in SMS Marketing?" Tatango, accessed June 4, 2022, https://www.tatango.com/resources/qa-videos/do-messaging-speeds-matter-in-text-message-marketing/.

8. Ilma Ibrisevic, "23 Ways to Raise Money for Your Political Fundraising Campaign," Donorbox, April 22, 2022, https://donorbox.org/nonprofit-blog/political-fundraising-ideas.

9. "How Political Organizations Use A2P Messaging to Win Campaigns," Tatango, September 2, 2021, https://www.tatango.com/blog/how-political-organizations-use-a2p-messaging-to-win-campaigns/.

10. Kimberly Adams, "Small-Dollar Donors Are Playing a Much Bigger Role in This Year's Campaigns," Marketplace, October 6, 2020, https://www.marketplace.org/2020/10/06/small-dollar-donors-playing-much-bigger-role-in-2020-campaigns/https://www.marketplace.org/2020/10/06/small-dollar-donors-playing-much-bigger-role-in-2020-campaigns/.

CHAPTER 8

1. "End Citizens United PAC," Ballotpedia, accessed June 16, 2022, https://ballotpedia.org/End_Citizens_United_PAC.

2. "Making Independent Expenditures," Federal Election Commission, accessed June 6, 2022, https://www.fec.gov/help-candidates-and-committees/making-independent-expenditures/.

3. "PACs and Super PACs," Ballotpedia, accessed June 16, 2022, https://ballotpedia.org/PACs_and_Super_PACs.

4. Tom Murse, "The Era of the Super PAC in American Politics," ThoughtCo., August 6, 2020, https://www.thoughtco.com/what-is-a-super-pac-3367928.

5. Idrees Kahloon, "Does Money Matter?" *Harvard Magazine*, July–August 2016, https://www.harvardmagazine.com/2016/07/does-money-matter.

6. "'Scam PACs' Are on the Rise: Don't Confuse Them for Legitimate Charities," charitywatch.org, Jun 17, 2020, https://www.charitywatch.org/charity-donating-articles/scam-pacs-are-on-the-rise-dont-confuse-them-for-legitimate-charities.

7. Julie Patel, "Super PAC Leaders Score Perks From Political Donations," The Center for Public Integrity, April 15, 2014, https://publicintegrity.org/politics/super-pac-leaders-score-perks-from-political-donations/.

8. Patel, "Super PAC Leaders Score Perks From Political Donations."

9. Sheila Krumholz, "Some Consultants See a Payday in Super PACs," October 20, 2014, in *Marketplace*, hosted by Kai Ryssdal, podcast, 4:07, https://www.marketplace.org/2014/10/20/some-consultants-see-payday-super-pacs/.

10. Ian Vandewalker, "Since Citizens United, a Decade of Super PACs," Brennan Center for Justice, January 14, 2020, https://www.brennancenter.org/our-work/analysis-opinion/citizens-united-decade-super-pacs.

11. "Super PACs," OpenSecrets, accessed June 4, 2022, https://www.opensecrets.org/political-action-committees-pacs/super-pacs/2022.

12. Eliza Newlin Carney, "Super PAC, Outside Spending Chiefs Make Big Bucks," *Roll Call*, January 14, 2014, https://rollcall.com/2014/01/14/super-pac-outside-spending-chiefs-make-big-bucks.

13. Frank Wright, PhD, in communication with the author, December 2021.

14. "Reelection Rates Over the Years," OpenSecrets, accessed June 16, 2022, https://www.opensecrets.org/elections-overview/reelection-rates.

CHAPTER 9

1. "Viguerie Book TAKEOVER Rockets to #1 on Amazon Political Parties List," PR Newswire, April 9, 2014, https://www.prnewswire.com/news-releases/

viguerie-book-takeover-rockets-to-1-on-amazon-political-parties-list-254555191.html.

2. Mandi Cai and Sneha Dey, "Nearly 18% of Registered Texas Voters Cast 2022 Primary Ballots," Texas Tribune, February 14, 2022, https://www.texastribune.org/2022/02/14/texas-primary-voting-turnout/.

3. Kahloon, "Does Money Matter?"

4. Kahloon, "Does Money Matter?"

5. Ian Millheiser, "Super PACs Pay Up to Six Times as Much to Run TV Ads as Actual Campaigns," Think Progress, September 25, 2012, accessed June 4, 2022, https://archive.thinkprogress.org/super-pacs-pay-up-to-six-times-as-much-to-run-tv-ads-as-actual-campaigns-b309c4edca3d/.

6. Bruce Mentzer, "Super PACS and Issue Advertisers Pay More Than Candidates. How Much More?" Mentzer Media, September 21, 2015, accessed June 5, 2022, http://www.mentzermedia.com/issue-advertisers-pay-candidates-much-lot/.

7. J.B. Maverick, "If You Purchased $100 of Apple in 2002," Investopedia, April 14, 2019, https://www.investopedia.com/articles/markets/021316/if-you-had-purchased-100-apple-2002-aapl.asp.

8. Jo Groves, "How to Buy Apple (AAPL) Stocks & Shares," Forbes, April 29, 2022, https://www.forbes.com/uk/advisor/investing/how-to-buy-apple-aapl-stocks-shares/.

9. Emmie Martin, "If You Invested $1,000 in Apple at its IPO, Here's How Much Money You'd Have Now," CNBC, December 12, 2018, https://www.cnbc.com/2018/11/01/how-much-a-1000-dollar-investment-in-apple-at-its-ipo-would-be-worth-now.html.

CHAPTER 10

1. Rudyard Kipling, "If," Rewards and Fairies, (New York: Doubleday, Page & Co., 1910).

2. Corrie ten Boom, Tramp for the Lord (Fort Washington, PA: CLC Publications, 2011), 56–57.

3. Rebecca Winthrop, "The Need for Civic Education in 21st-Century Schools," Brookings, June 4, 2020, https://www.brookings.edu/policy2020/bigideas/the-need-for-civic-education-in-21st-century-schools/.

4. Adam McCann, "Most & Least Politically Engaged States," WalletHub, October 13, 2020, https://wallethub.com/edu/most-least-politically-engaged-states/7782.

5. Drew Desilver, "In Past Elections, U.S. Trailed Most Developed Countries in Voter Turnout," Pew Research Center, November 3, 2020, https://www.pewresearch.org/fact-tank/2020/11/03/.

6. "Amachi Program: Mentoring for Children With Incarcerated Parents," Big Brothers Big Sisters of America, accessed June 16, 2022, https://www.bbbs.org/amachi/.

7. Thomas Reese, "Repealing the Johnson Amendment: Legal and Ecclesiological Problems," *National Catholic Reporter*, February 9, 2017, https://www.ncronline.org/blogs/faith-and-justice/repealing-johnson-amendment-legal-and-ecclesiological-problems#.WJ1QCteuBjM.twitter.

8. Deirdre Dessingue Halloran and Kevin M. Kearney, "Federal Tax Code Restrictions on Church Political Activity," *Catholic Lawyer* 38, no. 2 (1998): 107, https://scholarship.law.stjohns.edu/tcl/vol38/iss2/4/.

9. "Washington's Farewell Address to the People of the United States," govinfo, accessed June 7, 2022, https://www.govinfo.gov/content/pkg/GPO-CDOC-106sdoc21/pdf/GPO-CDOC-106sdoc21.pdf.

10. Billy Epperhart, "Kingdom Mindset: What It Is and Why You Need One," Truth & Liberty Coalition, accessed June 5, 2022, https://truthandliberty.net/2021/07/kingdom-mindset-what-it-is-and-why-you-need-one/.

CHAPTER 11

1. Ron Pierce, in communication with the author.

2. Pierce, in communication with the author.

3. "What Is the Firefighter Turnout Gear Temperature Rating (Heat Rating)?" Fire End, April 20, 2021, https://www.fire-end.com/blog/2021/04/20/what-is-the-firefighter-turnout-gear-temperature-rating-heat-rating/.

4. "William Borden—No Reserves. No Retreats. No Regrets," Southern Nazarene University, accessed June 5, 2022, http://home.snu.edu/~hculbert/regret.htm.

5. Sara Cain, "Hinds Feet," Hearts Being Healed Ministries, May 19, 2019, https://heartsbeinghealed.org/hinds-feet/#:~:text=A%20hind%20is%20a%20female,difficult%20terrain%20to%20elude%20predators.

6. "Perceptions of Citizen Advocacy on Capitol Hill," Congressional Management Foundation, accessed June 5, 2022, https://www.congressfoundation.org/projects/communicating-with-congress/perceptions-of-citizen-advocacy-on-capitol-hill.

7. Katie Bascuas, "Heading to the Hill? Follow These Tips for Your Meeting With a Lawmaker," *Associations Now, December 3, 2014,* https://associationsnow.com/2014/12/heading-hill-follow-tips-meeting-lawmaker/.

8. "Face-to-Face with Congress: Before, During, and After Meetings with Legislators," Congressional Management Foundation, accessed June 5, 2022, http://www.congressfoundation.org/storage/documents/CMF_Pubs/cmf-face-to-face-with-congress.pdf.

9. "Face-to-Face with Congress: Before, During, and After Meetings with Legislators," Congressional Management Foundation, accessed June 5, 2022, https://www.readkong.com/page/face-to-face-with-congress-before-during-and-after-9452154.

CHAPTER 12

1. Drew Desilver, "U.S. Population Keeps Growing, but House of Representatives Is Same Size as in Taft Era," Pew Research Center, May 31, 2018, https://www.pewresearch.org/fact-tank/2018/05/31/.

2. Desilver, "U.S. Population Keeps Growing, but House of Representatives Is Same Size as in Taft Era."

3. Lee Drutman and Timothy M. Lapira, "Capacity for What? Legislative Capacity Regimes in Congress and the Possibilities for Reform," in *Congress Overwhelmed: The Decline in Congressional Capacity and Prospects for Reform*, ed. Kevin R. Kosar, Lee Drutman and Timothy M. LaPira (Chicago and London: University of Chicago Press, 2020), 11.

4. "Congressional Staffers' Job Satisfaction, Career Trajectories, and Compensation," New America, accessed June 16, 2022, https://www.newamerica.org/political-reform/reports/congressional-brain-drain/congressional-staffers-job-satisfaction-career-trajectories-and-compensation/.

5. Scot Faulkner, "About," LinkedIn, accessed June 6, 2022, https://www.linkedin.com/in/sfaulkner/.

6. "Scot Faulkner Biography," Scot Faulkner, accessed June 6, 2020, https://www.scotfaulkner.com/biography.php.

7. "In His 'Meditationes Sacrae' Francis Bacon Writes 'Ipsa Scientia Potestas Est' (Knowledge Is Power)," Jeremy Norman's HistoryofInformation.com, accessed June 9, 2022, https://www.historyofinformation.com/detail.php?id=5253.

8. "Face-to-Face with Congress: Before, During, and After Meetings with Legislators," Congressional Management Foundation, accessed June 5, 2022, http://www.congressfoundation.org/storage/documents/CMF_Pubs/cmf-face-to-face-with-congress.pdf.

CHAPTER 13

1. W. Cleon Skousen, *The Five Thousand Year Leap* (Washington, DC: The National Center for Constitutional Studies, 1981), 5–6.

2. Benjamin Franklin, "Franklin to Messrs, the Abbes Chalut, and Arnaud, April 17, 1787," Pondering

Principles, accessed June 16, 2022, https://
ponderingprinciples.com/quotes/franklin/.

3. Bruce Ashford, "The (Religious) Problem with Socialism,"
The Ethics & Religious Liberty Commission of the
Southern Baptist Convention, January 18, 2016, https://
erlc.com/resource-library/articles/the-religious-problem-
with-socialism/.

4. "About," Victims of Communism Memorial Foundation,
accessed June 16, 2022, https://victimsofcommunism.org/
about/; Stephane Courtois, Nicolas Werth, Jean-Louis
Panne, Andrzej Packowski, Karel Bartosek, and Jean-
Louis Margolin, *The Black Book of Communism: Crimes,
Terror, Repression 4*, trans. Jonathan Murphy and Mark
Kramer (Cambridge, MA: Harvard University Press,
1999).

5. *2020 Report on International Religious Freedom:
Venezuela* (Office of International Religious Freedom,
US Department of State, May 12, 2021), https://www.
state.gov/reports/2020-report-on-international-religious-
freedom/venezuela/.

6. "Breitbart News Sunday—Sen. Rand Paul," Breitbart,
October 13, 2019, https://soundcloud.com/breitbart/
breitbart-news-sunday-sen-rand-paul-october-13-2019.

7. Tim Arango, "For Second Straight Year, California Sees
a Population Decline," *New York Times*, May 4, 2022,
https://www.nytimes.com/2022/05/04/us/california-
population-decline.html.

8. Robert Frank, "Tax Hike on California Millionaires
Would Create 54% Tax Rate," CNBC, July 30, 2020,
https://www.cnbc.com/2020/07/30/tax-hike-on-
california-millionaires-would-create-54percent-tax-rate.
html.

9. Skousen, *The Five Thousand Year Leap*, 7.

10. Interview with Jan Jekielek, "American Thought Leaders,"
Epoch Times, August 3, 2021, https://www.theepochtimes.
com/whole-foods-ceo-john-mackey-on-the-siren-

call-of-socialism-and-why-businesses-should-stay-apolitical_3931934.html.

11. Miles Cohen, "Capitalism, Socialism, Communism, and the Difference Between Social Democracy and Democratic Socialism," *Arcadia Political Review*, February 2, 2020, http://www.wesleyanarcadia.com/fall-2019/2020/2/2/capitalism-socialism-communism-and-the-difference-between-social-democracy-and-democratic-socialism.

12. Cohen, "Capitalism, Socialism, Communism, and the Difference Between Social Democracy and Democratic Socialism."

13. Cohen, "Capitalism, Socialism, Communism, and the Difference Between Social Democracy and Democratic Socialism."

14. Tomasz Kamusella, "How China Combined Authoritarianism With Capitalism to Create a New Communism," The Conversation, October 26, 2021, https://theconversation.com/how-china-combined-authoritarianism-with-capitalism-to-create-a-new-communism-167586.

15. Tomasz Kamusella, "How China Combined Authoritarianism With Capitalism to Create a New Communism."

16. George Barna, "What Americans Find Attractive About Marxism," George Barna, September 30, 2021, https://www.georgebarna.com/research/426832_what-americans-find-attractive-about-marxism.

17. "Fourth Annual Report on U.S. Attitudes Toward Socialism," Victims of Communism Memorial Foundation, 2019, https://victimsofcommunism.org/annual-poll/2019-annual-poll/.

18. Andrew Romano, "Poll: Half of Americans Now Predict U.S. May 'Cease to Be a Democracy' Someday," Yahoo News, June 15, 2022, https://uk.news.yahoo.com/poll-half-of-americans-now-predict-us-may-

cease-to-be-a-democracy-someday-090028564.
html?guccounter=1&guce_referrer=aHR0cHM6Ly93d3
cuZ29vZ2xlLmNvbS88&guce_referrer_sig=AQAAAIVq_
EJTZRoMCIWLgX-sEUicG-FgNmlOwxaxqB0262vj2CQ
A06fbXlTSGK2qYuL6E829E-0vKKeT4OdRQLqTign4r8_
E0Cn-AKqCJt5oCzb92M1GEM1mFbKcf8NzIj4cMSzBvT
1gZVTScXAYF2ANVCyfaN8dbMBZ_iMQ5BJCGdfW.

19. "The Dangers of Socialism to Religious Liberty in the
U.S.," First Liberty, March 20, 2020, https://firstliberty.
org/news/dangers-of-socialism/.

20. Maxim Lott, "How Socialism Turned Venezuela From
the Wealthiest Country in South America Into an
Economic Basket Case," Fox News, January 26, 2019,
https://www.foxnews.com/world/how-socialism-turned-
venezuela-from-the-wealthiest-country-in-south-
america-into-an-economic-basket-case.

21. "End-Year Report Regional Refugee and Migrant
Response Plan RMRP 2021—as of December 2021,"
ReliefWeb, May 13, 2022, https://reliefweb.int/report/
colombia/end-year-report-regional-refugee-and-migrant-
response-plan-rmrp-2021-december-2021.

CHAPTER 14

1. "Letters Between Thomas Jefferson and the Danbury
Baptists (1802)," Bill of Rights Institute, accessed June
6, 2022, https://billofrightsinstitute.org/primary-sources/
danburybaptists.

2. "Jefferson's Letter to the Danbury Baptists," *Library of
Congress Information Bulletin* 56, no. 6, (June 1998),
https://www.loc.gov/loc/lcib/9806/danpre.html.

3. "First Amendment and Religion," United States Courts,
accessed June 6, 2022, https://www.uscourts.gov/
educational-resources/educational-activities/first-
amendment-and-religion.

4. *Everson v. Board of Ed. of Ewing*, 330 U.S. 1 (1947);
Artemus Ward, "Everson v. Board of Education (1947),"
the First Amendment Encyclopedia, 2009, accessed

June 16, 2022, https://www.mtsu.edu/first-amendment/article/435/everson-v-board-of-education.

5. "The First Amendment Says Nothing About 'Separation of Church and State' or a 'Wall of Separation Between Church and State.' Where Did This Idea Come From? Is It Really Part of the Law?" Freedom Forum Institute, accessed June 9, 2022, https://www.freedomforuminstitute.org/about/faq/the-first-amendment-says-nothing-about-separation-of-church-and-state-or-a-wall-of-separation-between-church-and-state-where-did-this-idea-come-from-is-it-really/.

6. "About Becket," Becket, accessed June 16, 2022, https://www.becketlaw.org/#:~:text=Becket%20was%20founded%20on%20a,both%20at%20home%20and%20abroad.

7. "Religious Communities: Protecting the Right to Live, Teach and Organize According to the Dictates of a Religion's Faith," Becket, accessed June 7, 2022, https://www.becketlaw.org/area-of-practice/religious-communities.

8. "Churches & Elections—What Is the Law?" Texas Values Action, accessed June 7, 2022, https://freevotersguide.com/rights/.

9. "Religious Beliefs Have Greatest Influence on Voting Decisions," Barna.org, October 27, 2016, https://www.barna.com/research/religious-beliefs-have-greatest-influence-on-voting-decisions/.

10. "Religious Beliefs Have Greatest Influence on Voting Decisions," Barna, October 27, 2016, https://www.barna.com/research/religious-beliefs-have-greatest-influence-on-voting-decisions/.

11. "Churches and Elections—What Is The Law?" Vote Under God, accessed June 16, 2022, https://voteundergod.com/churches/legal-information/.

12. "Churches, Free Speech, and the Regulations of the IRS Regarding Elections – 2004," American Center for Law

& Justice, June 16, 2011, https://aclj.org/free-speech-2/churches-free-speech-and-the-regulations-of-the-irs-regarding-elections-2004.

13. "Tax Guide for Churches & Religious Organizations," Internal Revenue Service, accessed June 7, 2022, https://www.irs.gov/pub/irs-pdf/p1828.pdf.

14. Kelly J. Shackelford, "Churches and Elections—What Is the Law?" WallBuilders, accessed June 7, 2022, https://wallbuilders.com/churches-elections-law/#./.

15. "The Restriction of Political Campaign Intervention by Section 501(c)(3) Tax-Exempt Organizations," IRS, September 23, 2021, https://www.irs.gov/charities-non-profits/charitable-organizations/the-restriction-of-political-campaign-intervention-by-section-501c3-tax-exempt-organizations.

Chapter 15

1. "About Us," Isaiah 9:7 Movement, accessed June 7, 2022, https://isaiah97.com/about-us/.

2. "Eagle Small Groups," Eagle Forum of Alabama, accessed June 7, 2022, https://alabamaeagle.org/about/.

Chapter 16

1. Library of Congress, *Respectfully Quoted* (Mineola, NY: Dover Publications, 2010), 238.

2. Alan S. Gerber and Donald P. Green, "The Effects of Canvassing, Telephone Calls and Direct Mail on Voter Turnout: A Field Experiment," *American Political Science Review* 94, no. 3 (September 2000): 653, https://isps.yale.edu/sites/default/files/publication/2012/12/ISPS00-001.pdf.

3. Bryan Dik, "'God Doesn't Call the Equipped, He Equips the Called' and Other Half-Truths," *Relevant*, March 4, 2020, https://relevantmagazine.com/life5/god-doesnt-call-the-equipped-he-equips-the-called-and-other-half-truths-i/.

4. "'Government, We Worship God,' Says Trump at Veterans Event," CBN News, July 2, 2017, https://www.youtube.com/watch?v=FWTQgl4VSE.